PRACTICING MINDFULNESS

PRACTICING MINDFULNESS

75 ESSENTIAL MEDITATIONS
to Reduce Stress, Improve Mental Health, and Find Peace in the Everyday

MATTHEW SOCKOLOV

ALTHEA
PRESS

Contents

Introduction

AS MINDFULNESS AND MEDITATION PRACTICES have become increasingly mainstream, more and more people are actively seeking resources for how to incorporate these tools into their lives. But many of the existing books on the subject are centered on the *whys* of practice, including evidence-based benefits; they don't truly serve the beginner who's diving into practice for the first time. Many students have practical questions and share common concerns—everything from preventing the mind from wandering, to what to do if you really need to scratch your nose, to what you have to be, do, and have in order to "do it right."

There are a few practical guides out there, but even those are lacking in depth (and frankly, they're not very exciting to read). In this guide, I've drawn on my traditional training and my years of experience working with students to create a practical and straightforward approach to mindfulness, including a variety of options that cater to different personalities and lifestyles.

When I first sat down in a meditation class as an adult, I was struck by the fact that everyone in the room seemed to be completely at ease. At 18 years old, struggling with drug addiction, I had found a group of people who exuded a kind of calm acceptance that I could only dream of. At the time, my moment-to-moment experience was one of stress, chaos, and pain. I did not know exactly what I was searching for, but I knew I wanted to feel the way these people seemed to feel.

When I got sober a year later, I dived headfirst into meditation and mindfulness practice. I engaged with a local meditation community and began to see the ways in which I had been causing my own suffering and pain. Like all people, I've had painful experiences in my life. Some were caused by my own behavior; others were out of my control. My first big insight came when I realized that my *reactions* to these experiences were causing me more pain than the experience itself.

As the years passed by, my meditation practice became an increasingly important part of my life. I didn't have much money, so I attended a donation-based silent meditation retreat in Southern California when I was 19. For 10 days, I followed instruction and sat in silence. I felt massively underequipped and overwhelmed. I struggled daily with consistent thoughts of leaving early and constantly fought with the discomfort I felt in both mind and body. It was rough.

But when that retreat ended, I immediately signed up for another one scheduled a few months later. Although I never experienced a "white-light" moment, *something* continued to draw me toward the practice. Since then, I've attended ("sat") multiple retreats a year, ranging from seven days to four weeks.

Discipline has never been a strong suit of mine. It took a lot of effort to start meditating regularly, but as the months and years accumulated, I began to notice the benefits of practice showing up in my day-to-day life. Anger, anxiety, and harsh self-talk still came up, of course. But I found myself able to meet these experiences with awareness and patience rather than frustration and pain. Although I still had unpleasant emotional experiences, I didn't feel so strongly swayed by every situation or thought.

In 2014, I got the opportunity to lead some meditation groups at Against the Stream in Santa Monica, California. I filled in for the weekly Sunday group and was a part of an awesome team that taught a group for teenagers. In 2015, two of my teachers nominated me to teach meditation for a program at Spirit Rock Meditation Center, one of the most well-respected meditation centers in the West. This offered me the opportunity to work with inspiring teachers, cultivate my own practice, and explore what it meant to lead a meditation community.

When I opened the One Mind Dharma meditation center in 2017, I did so with one goal in mind: to create a space where anyone could come and investigate their inner experience in a safe, supportive environment. The community has done most of the work, showing up with vulnerability and honesty, and my role as the leader of the community is a powerful offering for my own practice.

When I first started practicing, I didn't fully understand what kept pulling me—I just had a faint notion that the way I'd been living was not working. I'd been fighting with every thought, resisting my emotions, and obsessing over past experiences and what I would do in the future. Without knowing exactly what it was that needed to change, I knew deep inside there must be a healthier way to live.

Like you, I'm human. I don't respond mindfully in every moment of every day. My brain goes on autopilot; I worry; I get frustrated. Today, my practice is to observe these experiences, remembering that I have a choice in how I respond. Before I embraced mindfulness, I was driven by instinctual and habitual reactions. But the more I cultivated awareness, the less enslaved I became to my fleeting thoughts and emotions. Instead, I can jump in and hit the Pause button, calm myself, and handle stressful situations with confidence and ease. In a sense, mindfulness practice has given me back my free will.

My deepest intention is to make these practices available to anyone who seeks a different, more balanced way of living. I have seen people from all walks of life turn to mindfulness for help with anxiety, grief, and physical pain. Regardless of *why* someone comes to practice, they generally all have the same goal that I did—to find a healthier way to be a human being.

When I was new to practice, the books I read, teachers I encountered, and classes I took gave me a blueprint to get started. Without those resources, it would've taken me even longer to incorporate a regular practice. My hope is that you can use this book as your own blueprint. I cannot give you a secret key to some advanced state of mindfulness; your work lies in curiosity, reflection, and, yes, a little bit of effort.

With a little direction, we all have the potential to live with more ease. May the exercises contained between these covers offer you a path to freedom in your life.

Mindfulness 101

WHEN I WAS 14 YEARS OLD, my dad gave me a copy of *The Miracle of Mindfulness*, a book by the Zen monk Thich Nhat Hanh. At the time, I was struggling with bipolar disorder and addiction, and the book offered a simple introduction to mindfulness practices, which my dad thought would help. As I read through the pages and practices, I was immediately drawn in by the beauty and simplicity of mindfulness meditation. I read each chapter carefully, seeking to fully understand the idea of mindfulness. Reading introduced me to the path, but I never practiced the tools offered in the book—I imagined that the principles would just seep into my daily life magically. It was years before I began taking action and seeing the benefits promised in the book.

I learned, as you will, that living mindfully requires a lot of practice. You don't start with perfect awareness and attention. First, you must understand *what* you are doing, *why* you are practicing, and *how* to actually practice. As you learn about the practices, try to apply them to your everyday life as much as you can.

Mindfulness calls for action. It calls for personal investigation.

People all over the world discover mindfulness as a tool to help with anxiety, anger, grief, and many other difficult experiences humans go through. This ancient practice has evolved over millennia and is now more accessible than ever. Every day, we understand more about what it means to be mindful and how mindfulness impacts the brain. By understanding what mindfulness is, how it may be beneficial in your life, and how to get started, you are laying a foundation for deep awareness and growth.

In the Moment, Every Moment

You have heard the word *mindfulness* before; it's featured on magazine covers, mentioned in fitness classes, and touted by top business leaders across industries as a tool to enhance productivity. But as mindfulness practice has become more mainstream, the meaning of the word has become clouded. People may encourage mindfulness, or "being present," but what exactly does this entail?

Mindfulness is often described as the practice of simply "being in the present moment." But this is only one aspect of the practice. Resting in the present moment is an important piece—it's the first step in bringing your attention to whatever is happening here and now, whether it's a thought, a difficult emotion, a task at work, or the breath—but it's just the beginning. When you limit your definition of mindfulness to the practice of just being present, you overlook several other important aspects.

As you move through the exercises in this book, you will see the terms *mindfulness practice* and *meditation* used interchangeably at times. The idea of sitting silently in meditation can be scary if you've never done it before. It is helpful to understand that the word *meditation* refers to anytime you are putting dedicated effort forth to be mindful. This may be in a sitting practice or while you are washing dishes. Remember that mindfulness is practiced not just on a meditation cushion; you can introduce mindfulness into any daily activity.

Mindfulness may be more completely understood as being present with clarity, wisdom, and kindness. If you bring your awareness to the present moment with judgment and anger, is that really useful? In order to build a healthy, beneficial mindfulness practice, it's necessary to cultivate several different behaviors, attitudes, and skills.

As you dive into mindfulness practice, you will likely discover a deep well of personal strengths—and a few places where you have room to grow. I call these places the *growing edges*. Try not to be discouraged by these edges—we all have them. Acknowledging and exploring them is how you work toward growth. Every one of your growing edges offers an opportunity for you to decrease stress and discomfort in your life.

NINE ASPECTS OF MINDFULNESS PRACTICE

You are here because you have made the decision to begin investigating mindfulness. It is a powerful step and one that should be recognized and appreciated. Take a minute to pat yourself on the back.

To begin your journey of understanding mindfulness practice, let's look at the different abilities you will be cultivating.

> **BEING FULLY PRESENT.** This is the most well-known and basic piece of mindfulness meditation, but it takes time to cultivate. You may have to coax the mind back to the present moment repeatedly as you practice. As you continue to train the mind to be present, you'll find yourself more naturally able to rest in present-time awareness.

> **SEEING CLEARLY.** This aspect of mindfulness may also be understood as a recognition of the experience you are having. When pain arises, you are able to identify it as pain. When anxiety is present, you recognize it as anxiety. You are cultivating the wisdom to clearly see what you are experiencing in the present moment.

> **LETTING GO OF JUDGMENT.** You may notice your mind labeling something (a feeling, a thought, etc.) as good or bad, right or wrong, positive or negative. In mindfulness practice, you can let go of such value judgments. When a judgment does arise, you can remind

yourself that you do not need to believe it. Accept what is present in the mind, including any feelings of "liking" or "disliking" what you find.

> **BEING EQUANIMOUS.** Equanimity is the quality of remaining balanced, especially when presented with difficult or uncomfortable circumstances. Whether the experience you are having is easy or difficult, the energy and effort you bring to it can remain unchanged. In this way, you build inner resilience, learning to move through difficult situations with balance and stability.

> **ALLOWING EVERYTHING TO BELONG.** Life contains a variety of experiences, and you may find yourself inviting some in while pushing others away. The English monk Ajahn Sumedho often tells his students, "Everything belongs." With mindfulness, you do not need to exclude any thought, emotion, or experience. Pay attention to whatever arises and make space for the uncomfortable moments.

> **CULTIVATING BEGINNER'S MIND.** When you learn something new, approach it with curiosity and eagerness to understand. As you grow in your understanding of the world around you, you can fall into "autopilot," believing that you know exactly how things work and what you're doing. To support a healthy mindfulness practice, work to cultivate beginner's mind, observing experiences and situations as if it's your first time. Remain open to new possibilities and watch out for the times when your mind begins closing.

> **BEING PATIENT.** Most people come to mindfulness and meditation practice with a goal in mind. They want to relieve some anxiety, deal with daily stressors, or learn to work through anger. It's okay to have an intention, but remember to be patient; clinging to a specific outcome can hinder your progress. Patience requires a little bit of trust in the practice, in your teacher, and in yourself. Keep your intention in mind and remember that growth takes time.

MINDFULNESS-BASED STRESS REDUCTION

In light of the recent research on the benefits of mindfulness, psychologists and clinicians are incorporating mindfulness into their practices at an increasing rate. In the late 1970s, professor Jon Kabat-Zinn of the University of Massachusetts Medical Center founded the Mindfulness-Based Stress Reduction program. MBSR is a form of mindfulness-based meditations and practices combined with contemporary science. It offers methods for reducing stress, helping treat depression and anxiety, and working with physical pain. In the past 30 years, MBSR has grown into a worldwide program with thousands of teachers and programs available.

In the 1990s, an elaboration of Cognitive Behavioral Therapy (CBT), Mindfulness-Based Cognitive Therapy (MBCT), was created to help prevent relapse in people experiencing depression. Therapists mix CBT methodology with mindfulness-based practices to bring awareness to judgment, self-criticism, and rumination.

Psychologists and psychotherapists have found success with mindfulness-based practices for a variety of individuals. Mindfulness-based relapse prevention is being used to help treat addiction. Mindfulness interventions have proven effective in working with post-traumatic stress disorder. And meditation awareness training can increase overall psychological well-being. As the body of research grows, so does our collective understanding of the practice and all its potential benefits. We are just beginning to scratch the surface of how mindfulness can help in clinical settings.

> **MAKING A FRIEND.** Mindfulness is not about beating yourself up. Kindness is an essential part of practice—and that starts by being kind to *yourself.* Without kindness, you can be reactive and unable to see clearly. When practicing, respond to your experience with gentleness. Act as if your mind is your friend, not an enemy.

> **HONORING YOURSELF.** You don't need to clear the mind, be perfectly calm, or be a master of kindness to start practicing mindfulness. Start wherever you are, and honor yourself for being here in the first place. This is a *practice*—not a race. You're not being graded, and if you struggle, it doesn't mean there's something wrong with you or your mind. Be true to yourself and allow space for growth.

The exercises contained in the following pages offer practical ways to build these qualities. You can return to these nine factors throughout your practice, recognizing where you have room to grow.

When I sat my first silent meditation retreat, I was struck by one thing that continued to arise in my mind: judgment. I knew from my training that I should seek to understand the judgment, not judge myself for judging. My retreat teacher suggested that I practice some kindness and forgiveness toward my mind. I really struggled with this—forgiving oneself can be a lifelong challenge—but I committed to an intention to do just that. Years later, this gentleness and kindness toward the thinking mind is an essential piece of my mindfulness practice.

You, too, will experience difficult moments in practice (and in life). You may need to try a few different approaches before figuring out what works best. Do your best to remain open, and remember to forgive yourself for not always having the answer immediately. As you continue to practice, you will deepen your understanding of what it is you need. You will know intuitively when to return to beginner's mind, when to practice gentleness, and when you are getting knocked off balance.

Research-Based Benefits

I recall participating in a meditation group in my teens, hearing a group of people share about the benefits of mindfulness in their lives. People told stories of mindfulness helping with panic attacks, curbing their anger, and encouraging a more compassionate lifestyle. When talking with them afterward, I found the joy and clarity in their eyes undeniable.

This was a turning point in my life and practice. I saw that mindfulness was a source of contentment and ease in the lives of other human beings. Today, we're lucky to have a body of clinical research to support that.

Mindfulness has been taught for over 2,000 years. People across the world have utilized its practices, discovering the personal benefits mindfulness can bring. We live in an exciting time—as scientific understanding has grown in the past century, many of the world's top minds are using modern methods to prove the myriad benefits of mindfulness meditation.

MINDFUL BENEFITS

Mindfulness has been studied in clinical settings, using brain imaging technology or extensive psychological testing. Although the field of mindfulness research is relatively new, research teams continue to find physical evidence of the anecdotal claims meditators have made for centuries. Many studies find changes in behavior and brain activity after just a few weeks of practice, with participants maintaining the positive effects up to a year after undergoing a mindfulness-based training program.

Understanding the research can ground you in why you're doing this practice in the first place and give you a glimpse at some of the benefits you might experience for yourself.

> **STRESS REDUCTION.** In 2010, a team of researchers analyzed findings from the past decade and determined that mindfulness was effective

in relieving anxiety and stress. This was true for study participants whether or not they had previously diagnosed anxiety or stress disorders.

> **IMPROVED WORKING MEMORY AND FOCUS.** Research at the University of California, Santa Barbara, has found that mindfulness helps people stay focused and more effectively utilize recently learned information. One encouraging finding of the study is that participants reported significantly less mind wandering after just two weeks of mindfulness practice.

> **PHYSICAL BENEFITS.** The physical benefits of mindfulness are well documented. Research in the past decade has found that regular meditation can help improve digestion, strengthen the immune system, lower blood pressure, help the body heal faster, and ease inflammation. Mindfulness is not just about taking care of your mind!

> **BETTER SLEEP.** According to Harvard Health, research shows that mindfulness can help with falling asleep and staying asleep. Regardless of what time of day you do it, a meditation practice is likely to help with this.

> **CREATIVE PROBLEM SOLVING.** In a 1982 study, researchers discovered that meditation can help people solve problems with more creativity. Cultivating stillness in the mind helps you gain the ability to think in new ways, look at problems from a different perspective, and work more effectively toward a solution. As a by-product, this can also help you deal with stress in the family, at work, and in everyday life.

> **FEWER FEELINGS OF LONELINESS.** Loneliness is actually correlated to poor health outcomes. In a study at the University of California, Los Angeles, participants experienced less loneliness after just eight weeks of mindfulness practice. This held true whether the individuals were

actually alone or surrounded by a group of friends. In addition, those who practiced mindfulness alone still experienced more feelings of connection and contentment. And in January 2018, after a lengthy investigation of loneliness in the United Kingdom, British prime minister Theresa May even appointed a Minister for Loneliness.

> **IMPROVED SELF-ESTEEM.** So many of us struggle with this. Mindfulness practice has repeatedly been shown to boost self-esteem across cultural boundaries. It can help you improve your body image, sense of self-worth, and basic contentment with who you are as a person.

> **MOOD REGULATION.** Although mindfulness is not a substitute for proper clinical care, it does offer a powerful way to help regulate mood disorders and issues. If you're experiencing periods of depression, anxiety, or mood changes, mindfulness may help you with these issues. Researchers have seen mindfulness help stabilize moods in those with diagnosed mood disorders and those without.

The Essentials of Practice

You don't need anything special or "extra" to cultivate mindfulness in your life. Getting started is usually the most difficult part, but over time, it becomes easier as you find what works best for you and your lifestyle. As you practice, pay attention to what feels easy, smooth, and "right," and what causes friction and resistance.

Use the practices in this book, the suggestions for getting started, and your own insight to help build a mindfulness practice. Throughout my years of teaching, I have heard of many ways to get started, and they're all slightly different—personalized to the individual.

Here are a few things you can do to help yourself get on the road to mindfulness.

When I was new to meditation, I really struggled to practice; it felt like a chore. But as I practiced more regularly, it became a habit. I even started to look *forward* to my periods of mindfulness throughout the day. As the benefits of my practice started showing up in daily life, my confidence and interest in mindfulness grew, and practice became even easier and more enjoyable.

All mindfulness requires from you is to show up and put forth a little effort. Below are the essential elements you'll work on as you build your mindfulness practice.

> **MAKING TIME TO MEDITATE.** With your busy schedule, it may seem impossible to find the time to meditate. In my experience working with individuals from around the world, this is a common challenge—and yet you can absolutely find time to practice. The key is making mindfulness a priority. A few things that help are setting aside specific time to practice, waking up a few minutes earlier than usual, or setting a calendar reminder to practice in the afternoon. You don't have to dive right into 30 minutes a day; start with 5 minutes.

> **CREATING SPACE TO PRACTICE.** You may struggle to find the right place to practice. Remember that this can be done literally anywhere. Let go of the idea that there are "perfect" places or "bad" places. You can also create a dedicated space for meditating—find an area of your home that is relatively quiet and relaxing. If your office or work space is too chaotic, try practicing in your car before going inside. You may also utilize public spaces, like beaches, parks, and quiet roads (if you're comfortable doing so).

> **SETTING AN INTENTION.** You wouldn't be here if you didn't have some intention in mind. Why are you interested in finding a more mindful way to live? Whatever your answer, it helps to consistently remind yourself of this deeper intention, connecting with what drives you.

The mind may try to convince you not to follow through, or that you don't have time to meditate. Fighting with these thoughts often proves futile. Instead, bring the mind back to your deeper intention. Remember what matters to you.

> **BUILDING CONSISTENCY.** The practices in this book present opportunities to investigate mindfulness in many different ways in your life. Try to use at least one every day, always keeping your intention of mindfulness present. Practicing consistently helps you train the mind effectively. When you practice every day, you build the habit fairly quickly. It's like going to the gym—if you go once a month, you probably won't notice results very quickly. But if you go twice a week, all those short little periods of exercise build on each other, and you grow stronger. Mindfulness is a cumulative practice; the mental muscle gets fitter as you continue training.

> **FINDING A FRIEND.** Social support can go a long way toward encouraging new habits. Try asking a friend or family member to practice with you once a day. This will give you a sense of accountability to someone other than yourself, and some external motivation always helps. You'll also have the opportunity to talk about your experience with someone else, which will help you both as you move through practice together.

> **KEEPING A JOURNAL.** Get a journal to use specifically for your mindfulness practice. After you practice for the day, take a few simple notes. How was your practice? Did anything new or interesting come

"Mindfulness is simply being aware of what is happening right now without wishing it were different; enjoying the pleasant without holding on when it changes (which it will); being with the unpleasant without fearing it will always be this way (which it won't)."

—JAMES BARAZ, *Awakening Joy: 10 Steps That Will Put You on the Road to Real Happiness*

up? How do you feel? The act of writing down your experience with mindfulness can help you understand it more clearly, ingrain your newfound insight into the mind, and give you something to look back on. I still look back at my first meditation journal from time to time, and I love seeing the progress I've made over the years.

Getting the Most out of This Book

This book will serve as a guide for your practice, offering direction as you get started with mindfulness. I personally use every practice described in this book and have seen them benefit my many students. You may find that some exercises or ideas are more useful to you than others. Remain open, trying each practice to see how it lands.

The exercises are offered in three parts: Basic Mindfulness Exercises, Everyday Mindfulness, and Mindful Moods. In each part, the exercises start short and simple. As you progress, the practices will build on previous exercises and require slightly more time. I recommend starting each section from the beginning and taking your time to master the simpler practices before moving on to the next.

If you are a beginner, I recommend starting with Basic Mindfulness Exercises first, no matter what your specific concerns are. This part details the foundational practices of mindfulness, and you'll continue to come back to them throughout your practice.

A word on meditation: Most people hear the word *meditation* and imagine a pious yogi sitting still for hours on end, with a completely empty mind. While seated meditation is certainly an important part of mindfulness practice, it's important to note that *every* mindfulness exercise in this book is a form of meditation, and there are plenty that don't require you to stop everything and sit quietly with your eyes closed. There are several more-engaged practices, various tools to use during your daily life, and many open-eye exercises. By incorporating both formal meditation and active mindfulness exercises throughout your day, you can lay the groundwork for a rich mindfulness practice.

ADDRESS YOUR ISSUE

Mindfulness and meditation are beneficial tools for almost anyone, and no matter what your specific issue, incorporating these practices into your life will have a positive effect on your overall well-being. That said, it is possible to focus your efforts on a specific issue, and that's how I've divided up the parts of this book.

If you have a specific difficulty you're facing, feel free to jump to those specific practices and sections. You can follow the exercises in the order I've presented, or skip around to those that call out to you or work best for your lifestyle and schedule.

HOW DO I KNOW IT'S WORKING?

Your first few times meditating may not feel very relaxing. It's incredibly hard to sit still and observe the mind, especially when you first start out. Like any other new habit, it will take time to see results. It's called a *practice* because it's not meant to have an ending—like crossing a finish line or cooking all the recipes in your favorite cookbook. Mindfulness is not meant to be a quick fix; it will keep you company throughout the rest of your life. As you progress, notice the moments of mindfulness that begin to pop up during your days. You can also tune in to any cravings for results (or a "cure"), and try to view these with curiosity instead of impatience. The early phases of your practice will help you learn to let go and trust the process.

> RELIEVING ANXIETY AND STRESS (see exercises 51, Calming the Body, page 119; and 55, What is this Emotion?, page 127)

> COOLING ANGER (see exercise 56, Cooling the Fire, page 129)

> WORKING WITH PAIN (see exercise 57, Smiling, page 131)

> MANAGING DEPRESSION (see exercises 61, Tender Heart for Others, page 139; 63, RAIN, page 144; and 65, You Can Handle This, page 148)

> EATING, EXERCISE, AND HEALTH (see exercises 29, Cooking with Clarity, page 73; 31, Doing the Dishes, page 77; and 35, Color Your World, page 85)

GROW YOUR PRACTICE

The practices contained in this book range in length from just 5 minutes to 20 minutes or longer. As you start the journey, give yourself permission to grow into the longer exercises. As you master the quicker, simpler techniques, your understanding and insight will build, and you can move on to some of the longer ones. This is a path of growth. Be patient with yourself, and move through the exercises at your own speed. I encourage you to try all of the exercises so you can experience all the different ways you can cultivate mindfulness.

EXTEND YOURSELF

Moving through the book, you will face challenges and difficulties. Some exercises will come naturally, while others may expose growing edges and require more time and effort. Remember, you are capable. You may doubt yourself in certain moments, but sometimes growth pushes you out of your comfort zone. These practices may lovingly nudge you to dig deeper. It is okay to experience fear, doubt, or judgment. Just keep moving forward with your practice.

Definitions

You'll see the following terms peppered throughout the exercises.

FEELING TONE: The experience of something as pleasant, unpleasant, or neutral. For example, the feeling tone of hearing a bird chirp may be pleasant, while the feeling tone of an itch may be unpleasant.

GROWING EDGES: The places where we have room to grow. These are often difficult moments where we struggle, yet we have a powerful opportunity to learn.

HOOKED IN and UNHOOKING: Hooking in is when we become enveloped in an experience and lose the power to choose how we respond. Unhooking is the act of releasing from the experience and returning to awareness.

LOVING-KINDNESS: The practice and quality of caring for the well-being of others. Loving-kindness is an opening of the heart, meeting others with kindness. Sometimes also referred to as *metta*.

MANTRA/PHRASE: Phrases and mantras are used in some practices as an object of awareness. A phrase or mantra is a simple sentence used to cultivate an intention, and it serves as a way to stay focused on a goal.

MEDITATION: Meditation is simply the act of dedicating time to develop a quality of mind or heart, often in silence. Though often done in a sitting practice, meditation may also be done while walking, doing dishes, or eating.

MONKEY MIND: The mental state in which the mind bounces around quickly, much as a monkey does from branch to branch.

NOTING: The practice of mentally saying what we are experiencing. Noting involves silently saying something in our head; it helps us see something clearly without getting hooked in.

PARASYMPATHETIC NERVOUS SYSTEM: The part of the central nervous system responsible for downregulation, including slowing the heart rate, relaxing muscles, and increasing gland activity.

PRESENT-TIME EXPERIENCE: Whatever is happening for us in the present moment. The present-time experience is what is arising into our experience on a moment-to-moment basis. It is always changing, full of different stimuli, and consistently present.

SENSE-DOORS: The six primary senses that can be accessed in our mindfulness practice: smell, taste, hearing, touch/feeling, sight, and *thought*. The sense-doors are where we experience phenomena arising and passing.

PRACTICE REGULARLY

Whether or not you have an existing meditation practice, a few minutes of mindfulness during the day is beneficial. Incorporate a practice every day. That consistency will encourage the building of a habit and help deepen your practice. If you have a busy day, find a short exercise in the book—and remember, the long ones aren't better than the short ones; any practice is a good practice. The five-minute exercises will be especially useful as your practice grows. They help refocus you when you start to drift, and they can be a great way to reconnect with your original intention.

FORGIVE FRUSTRATION

Anytime you are learning something new, it's natural to become frustrated. You aren't learning as quickly as you would like, you take three steps forward and two steps back, or you completely forget to practice one day. Not being "good" at something is frustrating—which is why forgiveness and beginner's mind are such important parts of the journey. The path to mindfulness is not a straight, one-way road. It winds, there are stop signs, and you may find yourself taking a turn you did not expect. Return to forgiveness and curiosity as many times as it takes.

The exercises that follow will help you investigate your own experience. Clarity will grow. You will learn to respond with gentleness. But you will not be pulling anything in from outside of yourself. The exercises work by cultivating that which you already have. Within your own mind and heart are the seeds of kindness, patience, wisdom, and awareness. Water the seeds and watch them blossom.

PART ONE

Basic Mindfulness Exercises

Mindfulness starts with learning how to be present. The practices contained in this part offer simple, traditional methods of bringing your awareness to present-time experience, which is why I recommend that beginners start here.

The exercises will help you cultivate the ability to be here and now with patience, clarity, and strength. We will discuss how to bring the mind back when it wanders, let go of self-judgment, and respond with gentleness. Through dedicated effort, you will learn to train the mind in the art of awareness.

1

Finding the Breath

TIME: 5 MINUTES

The body is always breathing, and the breath is constantly moving. Your breath is not only the best place to start; it's a constant you can return to anytime you need a little centering.

In this first practice, you will gently find the breath in the body. There is nothing to figure out, there are no problems to solve, and there's nothing special you need to do. Constantly return to your direct experience of the body breathing. You are training the mind to be with one experience without distraction.

STEPS

1   Find a comfortable position for the body. Sitting is often recommended, as it helps keep the body awake and energized. You can also try lying flat on your back, or standing. You may sit on a yoga mat, meditation cushion, or chair. Find what feels comfortable and sustainable for a few minutes of stillness.

2   Gently allow the eyes to close. If you're more comfortable with the eyes open, try softly gazing at the floor or ceiling (depending on your position). Allow the eyes to relax and rest on one spot. The idea is to minimize distractions in your practice. ➤

3   Bring your awareness to the abdomen. Relaxing the muscles there, see if you can feel the natural rising and falling. Imagine the body is breathing itself. From the navel around to the obliques, notice the movement with each breath. Take a few deep breaths like this.

4   Move your awareness up to the chest. As you inhale, tune in to the expansion of the lungs and the rising of the chest. As you exhale, feel the contraction and movement. See if you can follow the feeling of the breath from the beginning of your inhalation through the end of your exhalation.

5   Now bring your attention to the nostrils. The feeling of the breath may be more subtle here. Try taking a deep breath to see what is present for you. You may notice a slight tickle at the tip of the nose as you breathe in. You may notice the breath is slightly warmer on the way out.

6   Rest your awareness on the body breathing in one of these three spots. When the mind wanders, refocus on the direct experience of the breath. Continue to observe the breath for a minute or two.

7   Wrapping up this period of practice, bring this awareness with you into your daily life. Stay in touch with the breath in your body to help the mind remain present.

THE WANDERING MIND

The natural tendency of the mind is to wander. Even the most accomplished meditators have wandering minds! The brain was designed to process information; it's just doing its job. Rather than seeing this as a problem, approach it as an opportunity to strengthen your mindfulness. Try to bring forgiveness, curiosity, and patience to these moments, and whenever your mind wanders, bring it back to the breath.

2

Points of Contact

TIME: 5 MINUTES

The body is always in contact with something, whether it is a chair, the ground, your bed, or the air around you. This offers a powerful way to tune in to your present-time experience. You can be mindful of these points of contact anytime—in meditation or throughout your daily life. The sensations are generally easy to feel, making this an ideal practice for beginners to mindfulness.

"Mindfulness is the aware, balanced acceptance of the present experience. It isn't more complicated than that. It is opening to or receiving the present moment, pleasant or unpleasant, just as it is, without either clinging to it or rejecting it."

—SYLVIA BOORSTEIN, *Don't Just Do Something, Sit There: A Mindfulness Retreat with Sylvia Boorstein*

1   You can do this practice in any position, but I recommend trying it while sitting. Close the eyes and bring your awareness to the posture of the body. Make any minor adjustments to help the body be at ease.

2   Begin by noticing the places where the body is touching something else. Can you feel the contact between your feet and the floor? Pay attention to the physical feeling of the feet. There is nothing special to do. Just observe how the feet feel in this moment.

3   Continue up to where you can feel the contact between your rear end and the chair or cushion. Notice the contact and pressure of the upper thighs with the chair. Rest your awareness here, mindfully observing what this feels like in the body.

4   Bring the attention to the hands, however they may be resting. Feel the places where the hands are touching each other, sitting in the lap, or resting on the knees. Focus on whatever part of the hand is in contact with something else.

5   Now see where you can feel the sensation of the clothes on the body. You can scan the body to see where this sensation is present. It may be easiest to feel the places where the clothing stops and the skin is exposed, such as the arms, neck, or ankles.

6   Finally, bring your awareness to the sensation of the air on your skin. You may notice the temperature of the air feels different on the palm of the hand than on the back of the hand. You may also feel the wind if you are sitting outside. There is no right or wrong. Be true to your own experience.

7 Finishing this practice, bring mindfulness to the points of contact during the day. Whenever you sit down, feel the body come into contact with the chair. When you stand up, notice your feet on the floor.

DEALING WITH FEELING OVERWHELMED

When you first begin investigating mindfulness of the body, you may notice several sensations grabbing your attention at once. To help keep your mind focused, try using a mental note or simple mantra while observing a specific place in the body. For example, while tuning in to the feet, think, "Feet. Feet. Feet." Or, if you think a command would work better (it sometimes does), try, "Feel my feet. Feel my feet. Feel my feet." Link the rhythm of the words with your inhales and exhales. Congratulations! You're using mantras—it's that simple.

3

The Power of the Mind

TIME: 5 MINUTES

The mind is a powerful tool. In mindfulness practice, you learn to train and work with this tool in an intentional, focused way. This practice lets you play with the power of your mind, showing you how to gently coax it in different ways. You'll also witness the mind's auditory and visual thinking patterns.

Bring some playfulness and curiosity to this practice, and try not to take yourself too seriously.

STEPS

1 For this practice, you will need to close the eyes. Take a moment to notice how the body is resting. Keep the spine as straight as possible and allow the muscles to relax.

2 With eyes closed, try to bring to mind the room or space in which you are sitting. Can you picture where in the room your body is resting? Try to visualize the room in your mind. Picture the floor, the walls, and any doors. See what else you can bring up to piece together the space in your mind.

3 Letting go of the room, picture yourself somewhere peaceful. It may be a beach, a forest, or wherever your "happy place" is. In the same way, picture the space around you. Try to bring up as many details as possible.

4 Letting go of the visualization, bring to mind a song or tune you know well. Try to hear the words or melody in your head.

5 Now use the mind to change the experience of hearing the song. Try to turn the volume down, making the song quiet in your head. Turn the volume up a bit. Investigate what it is like to slow the song down or speed it up.

6 Pause for a moment at the end of this practice to recognize the power of your own mind. With a small amount of effort, you can conjure up visualizations, play music, and alter the experience in any way you choose!

LOSING FOCUS

While meditating, you may notice your concentration slowly leaking. Sometimes you'll lose yourself in a long train of thought for several minutes before you realize you've done so. When you lose focus during any period of meditation, bring your attention back to the last thing you remember observing mindfully, and if that doesn't work, return to the breath. Noticing the mind has wandered off, you have the opportunity to train it to be present. Come back to your practice as many times as necessary.

4

Who Is Listening?

In mindfulness practice, the focus is often on the feelings in the body and the thoughts in the mind. However, tuning in to your other senses can facilitate a strong feeling of presence and awareness. Just as you observed the breath in the first exercise, you can use the sounds around you as the object of your awareness.

Sounds come and go throughout your day and offer a consistent focal point for your mindful attention—no matter where you live or what you do for a living, it's nearly impossible to remove *all* sound. During meditation, investigate the experience of hearing. You can also bring this practice into your life, pausing to listen closely to the sounds around you at any point during your day.

STEPS

1   Begin by finding a comfortable posture and allowing the eyes to close. Bring your awareness to the breath, but instead of focusing on the *physical feeling* of breathing, listen to the *sound* of the body breathing. Inhaling and exhaling through the nostrils, listen closely to any noises coming from the breath.

2 Open up your awareness to the other sounds present. You may notice sounds of cars passing, noises within your home, or sounds from nature. Whatever is present, tune in to it.

3 The mind habitually recognizes what it hears. When a car goes by, you immediately know it is a car. Instead of identifying and defining what each sound is, try to focus on the actual experience of hearing. Imagine your ears as microphones, just picking up sound. Recognize the rising and passing of the noise, how far away it appears, and from what direction it is coming.

4 As one sound grabs your awareness, tune in to it for a few moments. Experience the sound fully. Then, open the mind and listen for other noises. Hearing mindfully, continue listening, investigating, and opening up.

5 At the end of the period, return to the breath for a minute. Without forcing or straining, encourage the mind to collect itself fully onto the sound of the breath in the body.

6 Opening the eyes and moving back into your life, maintain some awareness of the sounds in your life. Notice the act of hearing during your day, and let it draw you back into present-time awareness.

DISTRACTING SOUNDS

During periods of practice or in daily life, you may find certain sounds to be distracting. Noises, like construction, birdsong, or people talking loudly, can draw you out of practice. When you find yourself distracted, make the act of hearing part of your practice. Try to remove yourself from judgment or criticism about where the sound is coming from, and imagine you're hearing it for the first time. See if you can remove language from the sound and refrain from immediately identifying the source of the noise. Notice any aversion that arises, but don't resist sounds you cannot control.

5

Eating Mindfully

TIME: 10 MINUTES

Now we're going to shift away from mindfulness of the body and mindfulness of hearing and jump into the senses of taste, smell, and sight—starting with the food we eat. The celebrated Vietnamese monk Thich Nhat Hanh offers these words: "Let us establish ourselves in the present moment, eating in such a way that solidity, joy, and peace be possible during the time of eating." Eating is an opportunity to nourish your body while nourishing your mindfulness practice.

"This is the real secret of life—to be completely engaged with what you are doing in the here and now. And instead of calling it work, realize it is play."

—ALAN WATTS, *The Essence of Alan Watts*

STEPS

1 You can do this practice in any position, but it is helpful to stay still while eating. This minimizes unnecessary stimulus and helps you focus on the experience. You can do this with any food. I recommend starting with something simple, like raisins, berries, or a few of your favorite vegetables.

2 Begin by taking in the food visually. Notice the colors, shapes, and sizes. As you look at the food, notice the urge to start eating. There is nothing wrong with hunger, but allow the cravings to come and go. Return to the sight of the food.

3 Next, investigate the smell of the food. Some foods may have stronger aromas than others, and you may have to hold the food up to your nose. Be present for the experience of smelling. When the mind begins craving, just return to the smell in front of you.

4 Before eating, take a brief moment to appreciate the energy that went into its production. People worked to grow this food and bring it to you. Nature provided nutrients, rainwater, and sunshine. Maybe somebody cooked, cleaned, or packaged it for you. Bring into your mind all of the energy from various sources that came together to create this meal.

5 Now, slowly pick up the food. If you are using any utensils, tune in to the experience of touch as you feel the utensil. Mindfully feel how the food or utensil feels in your hand. Is the food stiff, soft, cold, or warm?

6 As you put the food in your mouth, notice the desire to chew and swallow quickly. Instead, start by feeling the temperature of the food. Holding the food in your mouth, can you feel the shape? ➤

7 As you begin chewing, notice the texture of the food. Does it change as you continue to chew? Notice the flavors. You may have a hard time doing more than simply labeling what you're eating, such as "It's a raspberry." Try to dig a little deeper. Are there multiple flavors present? Pay attention to the changing of flavors as you continue to chew.

8 When you swallow your bite, tune in to the experience of swallowing. What does it feel like as the food moves down the throat? You may also notice the desire to quickly have another bite. Pause and notice if any flavor remains in the mouth for a moment.

9 You can continue eating like this, reminding yourself to slow down and be present. Continue to check in with the sights, smells, tastes, feelings, and thoughts that arise.

10 When you finish eating, allow yourself to feel gratitude for the food that is nourishing your body. Let the mind relax into a state of appreciation for the energy and life.

GROWING IMPATIENT

Mindful eating is an exercise in patience and requires some self-control. As you try to eat slowly, you may come up against a strong desire to begin eating more quickly. Normally, most of us start preparing our next bite of food while still chewing the previous bite. The foundation of mindful eating is to eat slowly. If craving takes over, just pause, breathe, and slow it down.

6

Scanning the Body

TIME: 10 MINUTES

Body scans are a foundational mindfulness practice used in many traditions. This practice was first introduced to me by a therapist, but it may also be found in Buddhist traditions, MBSR practices, and yoga classes. By scanning the body, we get to know the feelings we experience more clearly. The mind also learns to rest in the present-time experience and focus on what is in front of us.

STEPS

1 Sit in an upright and energized position if you're able to do so. Allow the eyes to close and make any minor adjustments to be comfortable. Take a few deep breaths, arriving in the present-time experience of breathing.

2 Bring your awareness up to the crown of the head. What can you physically feel up here at the top of the head? You don't need to fix anything, figure anything out, or make anything special happen.

3 Continue down to the forehead and brow. You may be able to feel the temperature of the air on the skin, some tension, or maybe the simple, neutral feeling of the skin. Whatever you can feel, tend to it with mindfulness. ➤

4   Move your awareness to the cheeks and jaw. Moving through the body like this, just rest your awareness, gently observing what you can physically feel.

5   Tune in to the feeling at the nostrils and upper lip. Although you may feel many things here, the breath is generally the most obvious. Feel the sensations of breathing with each inhalation and exhalation.

6   Next, move into the mouth, focusing on the tongue, lips, and teeth. Notice how the tongue is resting, the sensation of saliva, and any movement in the mouth.

7   Continue to move through the upper body like this. Move the awareness slowly through the neck, out the shoulders, and down to the hands. Rest with each part of the body for a few moments, patiently observing what is present.

8   Bring the awareness back up to the shoulder blades, and move down the back. Feel the posture of the spine, the muscles in the back, and any expansion and contraction as the body breathes.

9   Tune in to the front of the torso, starting at the chest. You may feel the clothes on the body or the breath in the body. As you continue down into the abdomen and stomach, you may notice feelings related to hunger or digestion.

10 Move through the pelvis and hips, down the legs, and into the feet. Notice the points of contact, the feeling in the joints, and any tension that arises.

11 When you reach the tips of the toes, open up to feel the body as a whole. From head to toe, sit with the experience of having a body. Try to feel the outline of the body, the posture, and the subtle changes as you breathe.

THE BEDTIME BODY SCAN: *Body scanning is one of the most useful practices to help encourage sleep. As a bedtime practice, you can do a body scan while lying down. Start at the feet, and slowly move up through the body. Feel the contact of the body with the bed, and focus on bringing gentleness to the body. Breathe into any points of tension, and allow yourself to naturally relax. Don't strain to fall asleep or relax. Try to move from toe to head with a kind awareness.*

7

Every Breath Counts

TIME: 10 MINUTES

Bodhipaksa, a Tibetan Buddhist author and professor, said this about concentration: "Concentration allows us to really enjoy what we're doing: whether it's being in the country or reading a book, writing, or talking or thinking. Concentration allows us to think more clearly and deeply."

When you first start practicing, you may find the mind wandering quite a bit. Concentration practice helps you train the mind to focus by giving it something to *do*. Like mindfulness, this takes time. When the mind wanders, you bring it back. Over time, the mind will learn to focus and let go of distracting thoughts on its own.

STEPS

1 Find a comfortable sitting posture on a chair or cushion. Straighten the spine, but allow the muscles to relax. Briefly check in with the body. Allow the shoulders to drop, soften the muscles of the abdomen, and invite in relaxation.

2   Notice where you can feel the breath in the body. It may be the abdomen, the chest, or the nostrils. For now, pick one place where you can feel the breath most easily. Rest with the sensations of the breath in this one spot.

3   Begin counting the breaths. Inhale and exhale with awareness, and count one. Inhale, exhale, and count two. Continue like this up to eight, then start back at one.

4   Remember that the counting serves as an aid to practice, giving the mind something extra on which to focus. It is not a competition or measurement of how well you are doing.

5   When the mind wanders, just come back to the breath. Begin back at one as many times as necessary. Watch out for judgment and let go of any harsh self-talk.

6   Continue like this, counting the breaths and building focus. When the mind wanders, notice it. When the mind is concentrated, notice this as well!

7   When 10 minutes have passed, allow the eyes to open. Continue with your day, noticing when your mind is focused or wandering.

SWITCHING THE COUNT

There are many ways to practice with counting the breath. Concentration is an important practice, helping establish mindfulness, focus during meditation, and greater presence in daily life. By making slight adjustments, you can keep this practice interesting and prevent the mind from going into autopilot. Try counting up to eight, then back down to one. Or try counting with each inhale and each exhale—inhale and count one, exhale and count two. You may also change the number to which you count. Investigate for yourself what is useful.

8

The Mindful Body

During mindfulness practice—especially when you're just starting out—the body can grow anxious, restless, or agitated. To help with this, you can learn to respond to those sensations with compassion and gentleness. In this practice, you will work to offer kindness and compassion to the body. You can use this method of calming the body during periods of mindfulness practice, at various moments in your daily life, or whenever you notice difficulties arising.

STEPS

1   Allow the eyes to gently close, and make any adjustments to the body that feel helpful. As you breathe in, reach the spine up. With the exhalation, relax the muscles. Take a few deep breaths like this to arrive in the body, invite in energy, and encourage relaxation.

2   Rest in awareness of the body for a few moments. You can use the practice of observing points of contact or scanning the body to help yourself settle. Don't force the mind to do anything. Relax into present-time awareness.

3 Connect with your intention to be calm and at ease. Although there may be tension, anxiety, or discomfort in the body, recognize your own natural wish for the body to be comfortable.

4 Begin offering a few phrases of loving-kindness to the body. These phrases serve as a way of connecting with our own intentions to care for the body. Try saying them slowly, connecting with the words and their meanings. You may try offering a phrase with each exhale. With the intention of cultivating care, offer these phrases:

> *May my body be at ease.*
>
> *May my body be healthy.*
>
> *May I be at ease with the body.*

5 Tune in to specific parts of the body that grab your attention. Whatever body part comes up, offer a few phrases of loving-kindness.

6 Open your awareness to any part of the body that is experiencing difficulty or pain. Recognizing the discomfort, offer a few phrases of compassion. Compassion is simply attending to pain with a tender and open heart. Try using these phrases:

> *May my [body part] be free from discomfort.*
>
> *May I care about this discomfort.*
>
> *May I be present for this discomfort.*

7 After a few moments of resting with the discomfort in the body part, open the awareness again. Where else are you feeling discomfort? Offer phrases of compassion again here.

8 Continue with this practice as many times as necessary. ➤

PHRASES AND MANTRAS

The phrases used in meditation serve as a method of tuning in deeply to an intention. They are a type of mantra, a repeated phrase used to aid concentration. If you decide to experiment with them, know that the traditional phrases used in this exercise (and throughout the book) may not feel authentic to you, and that's okay. You can—and should—create a phrase that lands as honest for you and your personal experience. I sometimes say "This stinks" when it's all I can say honestly. I also like "I love you; keep going." As you practice, rest your awareness on the phrases as you say them silently in your head. If you're in a space where you may do so, you can also try saying the phrases out loud. Experiment with different words to see what feels supportive, caring, and true for you.

9

Giving and Receiving

TIME: 10 MINUTES

The breath can aid your practice in many different ways, including acting as a vehicle toward peace and acceptance. This practice is called *tonglen*, a Tibetan word that means "giving and receiving." In this meditation, you work with the breath to help cultivate care and loving-kindness toward yourself and those around you. It is a practice both in mindfulness and compassion. As you move through this exercise, notice any resistance that arises. When the mind wanders, bring it back to the body breathing.

"Tonglen practice begins to dissolve the illusion that each of us is alone with this personal suffering that no one else can understand."

—PEMA CHÖDRÖN

1 Gently close the eyes and bring your attention to the present moment. Notice where you are. What can you feel in the body? What can you hear? Where are you? There's no need to do anything other than observe your present-time experience in this moment.

2 Bring your awareness to a location in the body where you can feel the breath. For this practice, the chest works well. Be with the body breathing for a minute, feeling the inhalations and exhalations as they come and go.

3 Start the giving and receiving with an intention of self-acceptance. As you breathe in, visualize yourself breathing in acceptance. As you exhale, let go of self-judgment. Breathe like this for a few deep breaths.

4 Begin offering yourself some ease and peace with each inhale. Let go of stress and anxiety with each exhale. You may try the visualization of breathing in a light of ease, while exhaling the darkness of stress.

5 Now inhale and offer yourself forgiveness. You do not need to go into any stories or rationalizations about this; just set the intention to forgive yourself. As you exhale, let go of resentment.

6 Letting go of the forgiveness and resentment, picture yourself surrounded by people you love. Return to the first part of working with acceptance and judgment, but this time, flip it around. When inhaling, take in the pain of others as they judge themselves. When exhaling, offer acceptance to your loved ones.

7 Continue to inhale the stress and anxiety in others, and give ease and peace as you exhale. Hold space for their stress, but don't take it on yourself. By *receiving*, you're just recognizing with compassion that others have difficult experiences as well.

8 Finally, inhale and tune in to the resentments these people have toward themselves. Exhale and radiate forgiveness for these individuals.

9 When 10 minutes have passed, allow the eyes to gently open. Let the body resume normal breathing. Remember, you can return to this practice at any point in your day.

ADJUST THE PRACTICE: *There are multiple ways to utilize this practice. Try choosing different difficult experiences and caring qualities to offer. You can also work with whatever arises. If you notice self-judgment arising, use that. Breathe in and recognize that you are experiencing self-judgment. Breathe out and offer the wish that all others are also free from self-judgment. This can help us not get lost in our own suffering or difficulty.*

10

Body Awareness

TIME: 10 MINUTES

The body scan you practiced earlier (Exercise 6, Scanning the Body, page 15) is a useful preparation for this èxercise. Instead of moving through the body, resting on specific parts, however, this is more of an open awareness that lays the foundation for feeling the emotions in the body and responding with compassion. As with the body scan (or any of these practices), you can return to this anytime.

STEPS

1 Find a comfortable meditation posture. You can lie down during this practice, but if you find yourself growing tired or falling asleep, sit up straight while meditating.

2 Notice where in the body you can feel the breath. Pick one spot where the sensation of breathing is strongest, and collect the mind onto this part of the body. You may try using a simple mantra of "In, out." For the first minute or so, give the mind some space to settle into practice.

3 Expand that awareness to the whole body. From head to toe, acknowledge whenever something grabs your attention. You don't need to seek anything special. Wait patiently with the breath for a feeling in the body to emerge.

4 When something comes forward, observe what you feel. It may help to use a one-word label, discerning where in the body the sensation is occurring. For example, note "knee" when you feel a pain in the knee or "chest" when you notice the sensation of the breath in the chest. Don't label *what* the feeling is; label *where* it is.

5 Tend to the sensation for a few breaths, and return to the spot in the body where you are focusing on the breath. Continue to observe the breath until another sensation pops up.

6 Maintain this practice of alternating between the breath and other sensations in the body. Each time your attention is drawn elsewhere in the body, stay with it for a few moments before returning to the breath. Get to know your body and explore its experiences with curiosity.

ADDING TO THE PRACTICE: *If you want to add to this practice, start with a body scan prior to step 3 in this exercise. This can relax you and help you get more in tune with your bodily sensations.*

PAIN IN THE BODY

If you have consistent pain or discomfort in the body, it may continue to call for your attention. No matter how many times you try to shift your awareness, you are drawn back to this one place of pain. When that happens, listen. Maybe this area needs some loving attention. Try to look at the pain with beginner's mind. Switch to a phrase of self-compassion for your body, even something simple, like "It's okay."

11

Mind Your Steps

TIME: 10 MINUTES

Walking meditation is a common practice in many Buddhist traditions, yet it has been largely lost in Western meditation culture. Acclaimed Buddhist teacher Jack Kornfield says, "The art of walking meditation is to learn to be aware as you walk, to use the natural movement of walking to cultivate mindfulness and wakeful presence." Just as you bring awareness to the body that is sitting in meditation, you can bring awareness to a body that is moving.

STEPS

1   To practice walking meditation, start by finding about 10 to 15 feet of space. You can walk inside your home, outside in your yard, or anywhere you can access enough distance.

2   Stand still for a moment and close the eyes. Feel the body's posture, the feet on the ground, and any movement you experience.

3   Open the eyes. Choose which leg will be stepping first. As you lift the foot, feel the bottom of the foot lose contact with the ground. Moving it forward, observe the sensation of the foot coming back into contact with the ground.

4   Lift the other foot and attend to the experience with the same awareness. Remember that this is both a mindfulness practice *and* a practice in cultivating concentration. When the mind wanders, come back to the feeling in the feet.

5   Walk 10 or 15 feet, and mindfully turn around. As you turn, notice how the hips, legs, and torso adjust to turn the body. Walk slowly, taking a step every three or four seconds.

6   You may try incorporating a simple verbal noticing practice, similar to a mantra. As you lift the foot, think (or say), "Lift." As you move the foot forward, think, "Move." As you place the foot down, think, "Place."

7   When you are done with the period of practice, stand still for a few moments. Moving out of the period of meditation and back into daily life, you can retain some of this mindfulness of the body.

FOLLOW YOUR OWN PATH

You can do this practice barefoot or with shoes on. Either way is correct; just see what works for you. If you plan on practicing for a longer period, try incorporating awareness of other parts of the body. Notice the muscles in the legs or hips, or feel the abdominal muscles working. When the mind begins focusing on something else, note where it went. If you are thinking, note "Thinking"; if something catches your eye, "Seeing"; when a sound distracts you, "Hearing."

To encourage the habit of mindful walking, begin tuning in to the experience of walking during your daily life. Feel the feet when you're walking to the bus or your car, around your work-place, or in your home. Walk slowly—slower walking requires more concentration. When you find yourself speeding up, use it as a cue to slow down and return to the practice.

12
Caring for Yourself

TIME: 10 MINUTES

The practice of *metta*, or loving-kindness, can help you respond to your own mind with friendliness. Unfortunately, our thoughts don't always do what we want them to, and the body may have discomfort. Loving-kindness meditation encourages us to meet those experiences with a caring and gentle heart. This helps us see more clearly in our practice and daily life. In loving-kindness practice, you are not inviting in something from *outside* yourself; you are tuning in to the capacity for care and love that is already present in your heart.

> "Your task is not to seek for love, but merely to seek and find all the barriers within yourself that you have built against it."
>
> —RUMI

1 Sit in a comfortable posture and gently allow the eyes to close. From the beginning, try to bring kindness to the practice. Think of the body with friendliness. Listen to it and see if you can move to get more comfortable. You don't want to fall asleep, but you can allow yourself to be more at ease during this exercise.

2 Begin by recognizing your own desire to be happy. Don't dig into stories about what might make you happy. Find this natural wish for ease and comfort for yourself. Try saying to yourself, "Yes, I want to be happy."

3 With this intention in mind, begin offering yourself phrases of loving-kindness. As you offer the phrases in your head, say them slowly. Connect with the intention behind the words, even if you don't feel them entirely in this moment. Use these phrases:

May I be happy.

May I be healthy.

May I be safe.

May I be at ease.

4 Find a rhythm with the phrases. You may try offering one phrase with each exhale or with every other exhale. As you offer the phrases, use them as the object of your concentration. Rest your awareness fully on the phrases and the deeper intention.

5 When the mind wanders, come back to the phrases in your head. Notice any feelings or thoughts of self-judgment or resistance to self-care.

6 Stay with the phrases for as long as you feel comfortable. I recommend starting with 10 minutes. ➤

NOT FEELING IT

You may not really "feel it" while cultivating kindness for yourself. In other moments, you may have overwhelming feelings of love and care. Release any judgment and continue to open the heart. This is a practice that helps us cultivate a *quality*. If the quality of kindness is not present in your meditation session, know that you are taking action to create this caring feeling in the future.

13

Unhooking from Thoughts

TIME: 15 MINUTES

Thoughts are part of everyone's human experience. You don't need to push them away in order to practice—learning to bring your mind back from its thoughts *is* the practice. But how do you let go of the thoughts once they've pulled you in? This exercise offers one way to "unhook" yourself from those thoughts and simply let them be. Without pushing the thoughts away or denying their presence, you can be aware of the thinking mind while remaining unattached.

STEPS

1 Settle into a seated posture and close the eyes. Notice the energy in the mind and body. As you come into a period of mindfulness practice, you may notice the energy of your day resting in the mind and body. The mind may be active, the body may feel worked up, or you might notice a bit of lingering anxiety. ➤

2 Think of a shaken snow globe, with all that energy swirling around. As you rest, the little snowflakes fall gently to the ground. Think of yourself as a snow globe, and every snowflake as a thought. In this way, watch as each and every snowflake falls to the ground. Do not force yourself to calm down; let it happen slowly and organically.

3 After a minute or so, bring your attention to the breath in the body. Choose one spot where the breath is felt easily. It may be the center of the chest, the abdomen, the shoulders, or the nostrils. Observe the physical sensation of the body breathing. You may use the counting practice from Exercise 7, Every Breath Counts (page 18), if you find it helpful.

4 Observing the breath for a few minutes, bring the mind back when it wanders. Stick with the snow globe visualization, and as thoughts begin to rise up, observe as they slowly settle back down.

5 After a couple of minutes of focusing on the breath, open your awareness to *include* your thoughts and your general mental state. Instead of returning to the breath when the mind wanders, *notice* what the mind is doing. You may notice yourself planning, fantasizing, "figuring out," or replaying past experiences. Whatever you observe the mind doing, let it be.

6 When you recognize a thought, what happens? Try not to encourage the thought, but don't push it away, either. Allow it to be, and allow it to go on its own. See if you can watch the passing of the thought as it follows its natural trajectory and leaves the mind.

7 Return to the breath and patiently wait until another thought arises. Notice it, watch the thought, and come back to the breath again. Continue with mindfulness of the breath and the thoughts.

8 Notice when you're lost in thought or when the mind wanders for some time. If self-judgment arises, notice that just as you would any other thought. You can always return to the breath for a few moments to ground yourself back into the practice.

MINDING YOUR MENTAL STATE: *Notice your mental states when they arise. If the mind grows anxious or frustrated, acknowledge that it has done so. Mental states like these may be present with or without concrete thoughts arising.*

SEDUCTIVE AND TRICKY THOUGHTS

The thinking mind can be cunning and seductive, and certain thoughts (or patterns of thought) have the power to pull us in immediately. Although you may be able to "unhook" from certain thoughts with ease, others may be too powerful. Recognize these patterns and what types of thoughts continually control your awareness. When you find yourself grasped by one of these thoughts, smile at the trickster mind and just keep trying.

14

Energizing the Mind

TIME: 10 MINUTES

During meditation practice, the mind can grow dull or sleepy. In this short practice, you will examine a few ways to bring energy and alertness to your mind. You can incorporate these methods into your other practices, inviting clarity into your meditation.

STEPS

1 Allow the eyes to close, and find a comfortable meditation posture. Begin by tuning in to the experience of the body breathing. Rest with each inhale and exhale as you feel the movement in the body.

2 To energize the mind, you will start with the breath. With the inhalation, breathe in a sense of energy and awareness. Reach the body upward, straighten the spine, and open the chest. With the exhale, let go of sleepiness and distraction.

3 After a minute or two, allow the eyes to open—letting light in can help us stay awake and clear. Continue practicing with the breath and notice any sights that grab your attention.

4 Allow a few minutes to pass, and stand up. With your eyes open, standing on your feet, you are inviting increased alertness into your practice. It's much harder to fall asleep standing up than sitting down!

5   As you complete this exercise, take a moment to shake out your body and get some energy moving. Feel the warmth in your muscles as you move and go back to your day.

RESISTING SLEEPINESS

During formal meditation, you may notice the mind growing sleepy. Practices like this one can be woven into your daily practice to help induce a more wakeful state of mind. If you notice sleepiness arising, do not deny that it is present. Recognize that your mind is tired, and try to refrain from judgment. Also know that the more opportunities you give the mind to rest in stillness, the less sleepy you'll become over time.

15

The Attitude of Gratitude

TIME: 15 MINUTES

This exercise comes from the Buddhist practice of *mudita*, which means "appreciative joy." It can be understood as simply "showing up" for happiness with a caring presence. As you train the mind to rejoice in happiness, you gain many benefits. You feel more fulfilled by joy, recognize happiness more easily in your life, and train the mind to treat happiness as an important experience.

> "Every time you take in the good, you build a little bit of neural structure. Doing this a few times a day—for months and even years—will gradually change your brain, and how you feel and act, in far-reaching ways."
>
> —RICK HANSON, *Buddha's Brain: The Practical Neuroscience of Happiness, Love, and Wisdom*

STEPS

1 Find a comfortable posture and invite in relaxation from the beginning of your practice. As you breathe, appreciate the life offered from each inhalation. With the exhalation, let go of any tension in the mind or body.

2 Bring to mind a time in which you recently experienced happiness. It may be something small, like seeing a friend, watching the sunset, or the simple joy of lying down at night. When you have something, allow yourself to feel the experience of contentment.

3 With the intention of cultivating gratitude, offer yourself a few phrases of appreciative joy. Keep the memory in your mind, and offer these phrases:

May my happiness continue.

May my happiness grow.

May I be present for the joy.

May I appreciate the joy in my life.

4 If your experience feels more like contentment or ease, you can substitute the words that resonate with you. You know your own experience, so be true to yourself.

5 Offer the phrases silently in your head, finding a rhythm with the practice. Focus your attention on the words, the intention of appreciating the happiness, and the feeling of contentment from your memory.

6 After five minutes, release the memory and the phrases from your mind. Bring to mind somebody else in your life who has experienced some happiness recently. Picture this person in your mind, smiling as you observe their joy. ➤

7   As you did with yourself, offer phrases of gratitude. Rejoice as much as possible in their happiness. Offer these phrases:

May your happiness continue.

May your happiness grow.

May I be present for your joy.

I'm happy for you.

8   When the mind wanders, come back to the phrases. You can return to the visualization of this person smiling to bring up the happiness, and start with the phrases again. Continue this for five minutes.

WHY GRATITUDE MATTERS

In our daily lives, we often do not truly appreciate the moments of contentment, whether they're small or significant. Instead, the brain latches onto the difficult and painful moments, or becomes obsessed with solving problems. With this appreciative-joy practice, you can retrain the mind to give weight to your pleasant experiences, however small. By continuing to practice gratitude, you'll notice happiness more often in your life.

16

Resting the Mind

TIME: 10 MINUTES

Throughout these exercises and during your daily routine, you may notice the mind growing restless or agitated. Although you cannot always control the mind, you can encourage it to be more at ease. Learning to do this will help you *respond* rather than *react* to your thoughts and emotions. This practice gives you the opportunity to train the mind to slow down when it becomes overactive, and helps you practice ease and relaxation instead of perpetuating those difficult mental states.

STEPS

1 You can sit upright or lie down for this practice. If you are experiencing anxiety or stress in this moment, lying down may encourage relaxation.

2 Take a few deep breaths. Inhaling, fill the lungs completely. Hold the breath for just a second or two, and exhale slowly. As you let the breath go, try to empty the lungs slowly and completely. ➤

3 Recognizing that you cannot control every thought that arises, connect with your intention to relax the mind. If thoughts are present, just leave them be. Offer yourself two simple phrases of kindness toward the mind:

May my mind be at ease.

May I be at ease with my mind.

4 Synchronize these phrases with your exhale, offering one phrase every time you breathe out. Hear each word and try to connect with your own intention to care for the mind.

5 When the thinking mind starts up, come back to the breath and the phrases. Even if you can say only one phrase before the mind wanders, you are still moving toward relaxation by continuing to practice.

6 Completing this exercise, allow the eyes to open, and return to the activity of daily life. Watch the mind during your day, noticing when it becomes uncomfortable or agitated.

SWITCHING TO COMPASSION: *The mind and its thoughts can become painful in certain moments. You may experience guilt, anxiety, or grief. In these times, the above phrases may not be appropriate. Switch instead to mantras of compassion. Recognize that it hurts, and tend to your pain with care. Try this simple sentiment: "May I care for this pain."*

THE STUBBORN MIND

Sometimes, the mind just won't settle down. The harder you strain, the more agitated it grows. If your mind is overactive and won't slow down, try instead to change your *response* to that experience. Instead of stressing to calm the mind, focus your energy on accepting that the mind is working overtime and on responding with compassion.

17

The Judgment-Free Zone

TIME: 15 MINUTES

The practice of *noting* is a foundational aspect of mindfulness. Popular in MBSR and insight meditation, noting allows us to clearly observe what is happening without getting hooked into the experience. This "nonjudgmental noting" exercise will help you practice separating your *judgment* of your experiences from the experiences themselves. When you begin to untangle the two, you start training your mind to let go.

STEPS

1 Sit in an upright position and let the eyes close. Using the breath, invite both awareness and relaxation into the body and mind. Breathing in, reach the spine upward and bring energy into the body. Breathing out, let everything go. Let the jaw go slack, drop the shoulders away from the ears, and soften the muscles of the belly.

2 Start opening your awareness to include any sensations in the body. Following the instructions in Exercise 10, Body Awareness (page 26), note where in the body a feeling is present. Mindfully observe that feeling for a few moments; then open yourself up to other experiences in the body. ➤

3 After settling into this practice for a few minutes, notice when the mind begins *judging*. The mind may label some experiences or feelings as good or right, and others as bad or wrong. Don't encourage or discourage these judgments; just notice them when they come up. Continue like this for a few minutes.

4 Invite the sense of hearing into your practice. When you hear a sound, recognize that you are hearing. If a judgment arises about the sound, recognize it but don't try to do anything about it.

5 Continue practicing with openness. Whether you are hearing, feeling something in the body, or hooked into a thought, remain aware of your experience. Whenever a judgment is present, name it and leave it be. Resist the tendency to push it away, but do not engage with it any further.

6 Finish with a few deep breaths, settling the awareness back into the body before opening the eyes.

JUDGING YOURSELF FOR JUDGING

With this practice, you are tuning directly in to your judgments. The moment you see judgment arising, you may habitually respond by judging yourself for having the judgment. (It's that trickster mind at work again!) One of the most useful things you can do when this happens is to laugh at yourself. The mind is a funny thing. Try not to take yourself so seriously.

18

The Four Elements

TIME: 20 MINUTES

This practice dates back over 2,500 years and provides a different lens through which you can examine the body. Because this practice may feel awkward at first, try to take some extra time with it. Give yourself space to drop in and deeply investigate these elements in your body. Try to bring an open mind, and see what you can learn about yourself. Remember that mindfulness is about seeing clearly, and looking at things from a new perspective can often bring that clarity.

STEPS

1   Settle into a relaxed position. Close the eyes, and bring your awareness to the places in the body where you experience contact, such as the feet on the floor, the hands in the lap, or the body sitting in the chair. ➤

2   Begin with the element of earth or solid form. Without thinking too hard about what this means, openly examine where and how you can feel solidity. This might be the structure of your skeleton, the chair you're sitting on, any places of tension in the body, or the weight of your muscles as they relax. Don't rush through these sensations or try to force them. When you feel the earth element in the body, stay with it for a few deep breaths. Continue this seeking, recognizing, and feeling for a few breaths.

3   After five minutes, switch to the element of air or wind. An obvious place to start is in the form of the body breathing. Where can you feel the air of the breath? You may also look for places in the body where you can feel empty space—the nostrils, the mouth, and the ears can offer insight into the air element.

4   When another five minutes have passed, shift your awareness to the water element. Tune in to any sense of liquidity you can feel. There may be moisture in the eyes, saliva in the mouth, or sweat on the body—or you can feel the flexibility of your muscles, the flow of your breath in and out, or even the pulsing of your blood.

5   Next, bring your attention to heat or fire in the body. This element is open to interpretation, so look for yourself to see what you notice. Perhaps it's the temperature of the air touching your skin, or certain spots on the body that are warmer or cooler than others. Watch for any experience of temperature, either externally or internally.

6   To wrap up the practice, spend a few moments in awareness of the body as a whole. As you breathe, feel the four elements working together to support and fuel your body.

CREATING A QUICK FOUR-ELEMENTS PRACTICE

To create a quicker practice from this exercise, pick one of the four elements to focus on. If you've been feeling especially anxious and scattered, the earth element can help ground you. If you're feeling stuck or stubborn, air or water will help loosen things up. And if you've experienced any situation where you feel powerless, try connecting to the fire inside.

This practice also works as an active meditation to use throughout the day. Connect to the air element through the breath or the breeze. While walking, notice the element of heat as the movement warms you up. All four elements are always present in our bodies and in the world at large. Give yourself the freedom to explore different ways of identifying and experiencing them.

19

Tuning In to Feeling Tones

TIME: 20 MINUTES

Whenever an experience comes into your awareness, you can look at it more deeply by acknowledging its *feeling tone*. Feeling tones are *not* emotions. A feeling tone describes what you're experiencing as pleasant, unpleasant, or neutral. A feeling tone can be attached to anything you perceive through the senses, including a thought. By noticing the feeling tone, you continue to deepen your insight into the nature of your experience.

STEPS

1   Settle into a comfortable sitting posture. As you allow the eyes to close, focus on the sensations of the body breathing. You may use the counting exercise (Exercise 7, Every Breath Counts, page 18) to focus the mind. Concentrate on the breath for the first few minutes, dropping into a state of grounded mindfulness.

2 Include the whole body in your awareness. As you did in Exercise 10, Body Awareness (page 26), spend a few minutes just noticing what arises in the body. Don't judge anything as good or bad; just pay attention to the actual experience of feeling in the body.

3 Once you are present with the bodily sensations, expand your awareness to include feeling tones. Acknowledge the feeling in the body, and consider whether the experience is pleasant, unpleasant, or neutral. If you like, you can do a body scan (Exercise 6, Scanning the Body, page 15) and notice the feeling tone for each place in the body.

4 After five minutes, include the sense of hearing in your practice. As sound arrives in your awareness, note that you are hearing, and observe the feeling tone. Continue with awareness of the body and sound for five minutes.

5 Finally, include the thoughts. You don't need to dive into exactly what you're thinking—recognize when a thought is present and if there is a feeling tone attached. Then open back up and wait for the next experience to arise.

6 Resting in open mindfulness can leave space for mental wandering. Remember that you can always return to the breath as your anchor during this practice. Don't hesitate to return to it for a minute or two in order to collect the mind.

7 Take a few deep breaths and open the eyes. Moving through your day, see if you can notice feeling tones attached to what you see, hear, and feel. ➤

BE OPEN TO CHANGE: *Feeling tones are not stable or fixed. In one moment you may find an experience to be pleasant, and in the next it may feel unpleasant. Remember to practice beginner's mind, remaining curious and open.*

NOT KNOWING

Some experiences may not *have* a clear feeling tone. Although we generally work with pleasant, unpleasant, or neutral, there are other options you can play with, as well. If you do not know the feeling tone, say, "I don't know." If it feels mixed, say, "Mixed." There's no use in straining if the feeling tone is not clear. Be honest, honoring your own personal experience.

20

The Emotional Experience

TIME: 15 MINUTES

Emotions are complex occurrences that can be most simply understood as a combination of physical sensations and thought patterns. When you mindfully tune in to your emotional experience, you can begin to break it down and separate yourself from its power. With wisdom and care, you'll become able to let go of your feelings rather than allowing them to rule you.

"You have a unique body and mind, with a particular history and conditioning. No one can offer you a formula for navigating all situations and all states of mind. Only by listening inwardly in a fresh and open way will you discern at any given time what most serves your healing and freedom."

—TARA BRACH, *True Refuge: Finding Peace and Freedom in Your Own Awakened Heart*

1 Find a posture that feels both comfortable and conducive to mindfulness. Although you may know what works for you in general, be open to any adjustments that can be made. Take a few moments to examine the body and what is present.

2 Bring to mind a recent experience of joy or happiness. Try to recall as many details as you can about this event. Visualize the experience, and give it space to be present in the mind and body.

3 As this emotional experience is with you, investigate it closely. What *is* this joy? Notice what you feel in the body. You may notice a relaxing of the shoulders, gentler or deeper breaths, or a warmth in the chest. There's nothing you should or should not be feeling; just recognize your own experience of joy.

4 Tune in to the mental state that accompanies this physical sensation. As you rest with the memory of joy, what is happening in the mind? Notice if it is calm, active, agitated, or at ease. There isn't a right or wrong answer. Familiarize yourself with the experience of joy.

5 Now, do the same with a recent experience that was unpleasant. It may be a time in which you were stressed, anxious, frustrated, or sad. Steer clear of experiences that are powerfully charged, like an intense argument or workplace conflict. Instead, start with something minorly unpleasant, like sitting in traffic or navigating a crowded grocery store.

6   Investigate this experience in both mind and body, resting with each for a few minutes.

7   Return to the body and the breath for a minute at the end of your practice. Allow the mind to relax for a few deep breaths before opening the eyes.

WORKING WITH OPEN EMOTIONS

Instead of intentionally calling up past emotions, you can do this practice with open awareness and work with any emotion arising as you sit. If you patiently wait with mindfulness, you have an opportunity to observe how emotions come and go. Recognizing the transient nature of your feelings can help you become less attached to them over time. You may also pause to do this during your day whenever you notice yourself having an emotional experience.

21

Grounded and Flexible

TIME: 15 MINUTES

Equanimity is the quality of remaining grounded and stable in the midst of your experience. When you notice suffering, you respond with compassion, and you don't get knocked off balance by the unexpected. With equanimity practice, you cultivate a state of mind that is both grounded and flexible, especially in the midst of intense emotional experiences.

> "A modern definition of equanimity: cool. This refers to one whose mind remains stable and calm in all situations."
>
> —ALLAN LOKOS, *Pocket Peace: Effective Practices for Enlightened Living*

1 Closing the eyes and finding your posture, bring your awareness into your present experience. Notice the sounds, the feelings in the body, and your overall mental state.

2 Open your awareness. When something comes up, tune in to the mind, noticing where you get knocked off balance. Certain sounds, thoughts, or feelings in the body may feel charged, pulling you from your calm state of mind. Sit with this awareness of your own balance for five minutes.

3 Bring to mind someone you care about deeply. Connect with your intention to care for this person. Recognize that although you may care for this person, you cannot control their happiness. Offer a few phrases of equanimity:

May you be happy.

May you be in charge of your happiness.

Your happiness is dependent upon your actions, not my wishes for you.

4 After five minutes, switch to somebody else you care about. Try to find someone who is currently experiencing some pain or suffering. Connecting with your intention to care but remain stable, offer these phrases of compassion and equanimity:

May you be free from suffering.

May you take action to care for your pain.

Your freedom is dependent upon your actions, not my wishes for you. ➤

5   Finally, bring to mind somebody in your life who has had some joy or success recently. Offer a few phrases of appreciative joy, staying connected to your equanimity.

May your joy continue.

May you be in charge of your joy.

Your joy is in your hands and is not dependent upon my wishes for you.

6   After a few minutes of offering these phrases, return to your own experience before opening the eyes. Recognize that your happiness is in your own hands. Be proud of your effort in practicing, encouraging happiness for yourself.

FALLING INTO APATHY

Equanimity has what is called a "near enemy." This is a quality that looks similar but is actually not helpful. The near enemy of equanimity is *apathy*—the quality of not caring at all. Whereas equanimity is about attending to your experience with care and stability, apathy is turning away from the experience altogether and ceasing to care. Watch out for apathy or indifference as you practice. If apathy arises, return to your phrases of loving-kindness, reconnecting with the naturally caring part of your heart.

22

Feel the Love

TIME: 20 MINUTES

This practice offers an alternate way to allow ourselves to be cared for. We will work with a technique of visualization in receiving love and care. This will help you cultivate the capacity to accept love and recognize your innate worthiness.

STEPS

1   As you find a comfortable posture and allow the eyes to close, make a special effort to bring kindness to your practice today. Relax the body and let the mind be at ease.

2   Bring to mind a person who cares for you. It may be a family member, a good friend, or a mentor of some kind. Picture this person standing in front of you, offering you phrases of loving-kindness. Your job is simply to receive their wishes. Continue receiving these intentions for five minutes.

3   Add another person who cares about you into the mix. Accept the wishes of well-being from these two individuals, allowing their care and love to land deeply in your consciousness. ➤

4   After a few minutes, bring in a third individual. Continue bringing others in slowly until you have a group of people in front of you, offering you words and feelings of kindness. Try to accept these wishes with an open heart.

5   When you come to the end of your practice, bring your own gentleness and care into your experience. Open the eyes slowly, and make your way back into daily life with patient kindness.

CLOSING THE HEART

The heart and mind can grow uncomfortable as they receive love. You may not feel worthy of the love or kindness you are receiving. Notice when and if the heart begins closing, or when the mind tries to distract you with stories. Try to tune back in to the felt sense of receiving love in the body. Work toward achieving an embodied sense of being loved.

23

Cultivating Concentration

TIME: 20 MINUTES

In Exercise 7, Every Breath Counts (page 18), you used breath counting to help build concentration in the mind for a short period of time. Dedicating longer intervals to this practice can help you deepen your mindfulness practice (and it's useful in day-to-day life as well). Starting with the counting of the breath, this exercise offers a few different ways to build concentration more deeply.

STEPS

1   After you settle into your posture, begin with the practice of counting the breaths. Focus the attention on the body breathing, and bring the mind back every time it wanders. Practice like this for the first five minutes.

2   Let go of the counting, but stay with the breath. Mindfully watch the breath with your full awareness, noticing if it becomes more difficult without the counting. Continue for five minutes. ➤

3 Now, switch to the sensation of hearing. Find a relatively stable noise in your environment. It may be the sound of a nearby street, the humming of electricity or lights, or the subtle ringing in the ears. Use your hearing as the object of your awareness. When the mind wanders, come back to this sound.

4 After five minutes, open the eyes. Find one object on which you can focus your attention. Look at it with curiosity, noticing every detail of the object—its outline, its color, its texture, and so on. When other sights, sounds, or thoughts distract you, return to the object you have chosen. Practice this for the final five minutes.

MONKEY MIND

When working with concentration, you may experience what's called "monkey mind." Monkey mind is when the mind is unsettled, jumping around like a monkey swinging from tree to tree. If monkey mind becomes distracting, open yourself up to the thoughts. Although you may start this exercise with the intention of building concentration, give yourself permission to switch to a mindfulness-of-thoughts practice. Recognize the thoughts arising, welcome them in, and don't push them away.

24

Open-Awareness Meditation

TIME: 25 MINUTES

This is a traditional mindfulness meditation, similar to what most people think of when they hear the word *meditation*. Using mindfulness of the senses, feeling tones, and your overall experience in the present moment, this is a practice in true open awareness. It is the cornerstone of mindfulness practice for many meditators across the world.

Open-Awareness Meditation is a combination of some of the shorter, more focused exercises earlier in this section. Throughout the exercise, rest in openness, receiving whatever arises into your experience.

STEPS

1   Start with a brief body scan. Moving from head to toe, rest your attention on each part of the body with mindfulness.

2   After completing the body scan, open your awareness to the sensations in the body—tension, pain, softness, the desire to fidget, or maybe an emotion or feeling. What arises and grabs your attention? Mindfully observe the body for five minutes. ➤

3   Open your practice to the experience of hearing. When a sound comes into your awareness, acknowledge that you are hearing. Sit for five minutes with patience, noticing any bodily sensations or sounds present.

4   Continue to open, this time including the thinking mind. You may see thoughts, emotional experiences, or general mental states. Whatever is present, note that you are having an experience of the mind.

5   Finally, add in the practice of noting feeling tone. Cultivate an intention to receive and remain open. Recognize whatever is present in your awareness and how it feels. If the mind is reacting to any part of your experience, make that reaction a part of your practice.

6   As you complete this meditation and move into daily life, try to sustain some of this awareness.

OPEN MINDFULNESS DURING YOUR DAY: *You can make this practice a part of your everyday mindfulness. Pause for a few moments during your day and start with the fifth step of this exercise. Open up to your entire experience, and spend a minute or two noting what is present. This can help bring you back to the present-time experience in stressful or boring moments.*

TOO OPEN

Open-mindfulness practice can sometimes feel *too* open. By allowing space for anything to arise, you may start to feel lazy or overly relaxed. As the mind relaxes, it may start to spin out on random trains of thought. If you find this happening, try tightening your awareness a bit by focusing on one of your five senses (hearing usually works well). Remember that every time you bring the mind back, you are strengthening the mental muscles of mindfulness and concentration.

25

Breathing and Noting

TIME: 25 MINUTES

This is an alternate way to work with open mindfulness, and it's how I practice every day. This combination of intentional concentration and open awareness is inspired by the Burmese monk Mahasi Sayadaw. *Breathing and Noting* is a popular practice among students of mindfulness across the world.

"Every time one notes an object well, it gives rise to delight. As a result of this, practice becomes enjoyable."

—**MAHASI SAYADAW,** *Manual of Insight*

1 Settle the body into a comfortable posture and allow the eyes to close.

2 Focus your awareness on the breath. You can start with a counting exercise if you find it helpful.

3 Choosing one location in the body, use the simple terms *in* and *out* to note each inhale and exhale. Continue for five minutes or more, until the mind begins to settle.

4 Staying with the inhale and exhale, bring your awareness to the body in general. After the exhale, note one place in the body where you can feel a sensation. For example, you may note the following: "In, out, foot"; "In, out, chest"; and so on.

5 After five minutes, incorporate the sensation of hearing. Continue to note the inhalation and exhalation; then note a feeling in the body or a sound.

6 Next, open up to the thinking mind. As you have been doing, continue resting with the breath. As you breathe out, open up to any thoughts, feelings in the body, and sounds.

7 Finally, include feeling tones. You now are resting with the breath and noting any bodily sensations, noises, thoughts, and feeling tones after each exhale.

ANXIETY AND FEELING OVERWHELMED

You may notice feeling overwhelmed or stress arising during this practice. Welcome it in and make it a part of your practice. You can try slowing the breath down to encourage relaxation, or return to the simple practice of breath counting to give yourself a break before opening the awareness back up.

PART TWO

Everyday Mindfulness

Meditation is a powerful way to ground your mindfulness practice and gain lasting insights that carry into daily life. However, you can't spend all day sitting in meditation. Bringing mindfulness to your everyday activities and responsibilities can help create a more consistent state of presence.

In this part, you will find exercises that help you remain present with kindness and wisdom as you move through your day. The more you practice this, the more easily it will come. Remember, this is a *practice*. It takes patience and persistence to train and retrain the mind.

26

The Awareness Trigger

One of the most difficult parts about practicing mindfulness is actually *remembering* to practice. For this reason, an awareness trigger can help you form a habit. You can incorporate this at multiple points throughout your day, experiment with different triggers, and use different methods of mindfulness with this exercise.

STEPS

1 In the morning, pick one task or event that is likely to happen a few times during the day, for example, the sound of the phone ringing, the act of sitting down, or seeing the color red.

2 Picking one event or behavior, set a clear intention to use this as a trigger for mindfulness throughout your day. Take a moment to connect with your goals and hopes for yourself, encouraging awareness during your day.

3 Whenever you notice your trigger, pause and practice a few moments of mindfulness. You can do any of the exercises from part I—working with the breath, observing the points of contact, or any other method in this book that works for you. ➤

4   After dedicating a few moments to present-time awareness, you can return to your daily life. Remember to continue bringing awareness to the present moment whenever your trigger arises throughout the day.

FINDING THE RIGHT TRIGGER: *There are many different triggers you can use for this practice. Give yourself the freedom to choose a trigger that's relevant and reliable in your lifestyle. If you work in front of a computer, you may try using the receipt of an e-mail. If you spend a lot of time outside, use the feeling of the wind on your face. Continue to adapt and experiment with different triggers until you find the ones that work best.*

27

Waking Up with Awareness

TIME: 5 MINUTES

One of the best techniques to help bring mindfulness to every-day living is to start your day with it. Many of us have a rushed morning routine and do not pause to be present until later in the day. This exercise can help you start off your day with a mindful moment, bolstering your practice in the coming hours.

STEPS

1   When you wake up, take a moment to pause before you get up. If you use an alarm clock, try attaching a sticky note to it to remind yourself.

2   Lying in bed, tune in to the body. Feel the body resting, and notice how it feels to begin moving and stretching.

3   Bring your awareness to the breath. Taking a few deep breaths, recognize that you woke up and are breathing this morning. ➤

4   As you get up and begin your day, try to retain some awareness. Routines make it easy to fall into autopilot. Notice when you lose your presence, and come back to mindfulness.

THE MORNING CHAOS

Mornings may be an especially chaotic time. Rushing to get to work, taking care of children, and dealing with the foggy morning brain can make it difficult to really be present. This calls for extra effort and kindness. The places and times that give you trouble are often the richest opportunities to practice. Notice when your mind and body are moving toward stress. You don't need to do anything; watch it happen with patient awareness. Just observing this process can help you understand it more deeply and become less vulnerable to it in the future.

28

The Creative Flow

Taking the time to be creative during your day can build lasting benefits in all areas of your life. Creativity can boost self-awareness, relieve stress, and help you solve problems more easily. In addition, you can cultivate mindfulness while indulging your creative side. Do this exercise with your activity of choice, and remember that you can pause at any time and use this technique to encourage present-time awareness.

STEPS

1   Get a blank piece of paper and a pen. If you want to use crayons, markers, or colored pencils, that is even better. Set aside 10 minutes, perhaps setting a timer if it helps you really dedicate the time to practice.

2   Bring your awareness to your experience in this moment. Feel the pen in the hand, see the piece of paper, and notice any thoughts going through the mind. If judgment arises about your creative talents, notice them as they come up. ➤

3   Start drawing. You don't need to create a masterpiece. There is nothing wrong with stick figures and doodles. Draw whatever you want. It may be a happy memory, scenery, or something you can see right now.

4   As you draw, notice what you are drawing. If it's a person, note that you're drawing a person. If there is movement, notice there is movement. Watch for any emotions that arise, exploring whether the piece is happy, sad, fun, beautiful, and so on.

5   Take special care to watch for judgments. However creative you consider yourself to be, you may find the mind telling you that you're no good. Thank the mind for these contributions and continue drawing.

6   After 10 minutes, put down the pen. Look at what you've drawn, and take it in. Examine the lines, figures, and overall piece. Again, notice the thoughts and judgments when they arise. You may choose to save the piece, or not—the activity is the point, not the result.

CREATIVE OUTLETS: *This exercise will work with any form of creativity. Try filling in a coloring book, taking photos, playing an instrument, or dancing. The only limits are the ones you put on yourself! Allow yourself just 10 minutes of freedom from judgment, and follow your passion.*

29

Cooking with Clarity

TIME: 15 MINUTES

Cooking or preparing a meal is an opportunity to form a loving connection with your food. As you prepare a meal, you can cultivate mindfulness of your body and mind as well as the food you will be eating. Whether you're making a quick meal or preparing a feast, use this exercise to ground yourself in the present moment.

> "Cooking is at once child's play and adult joy. And cooking done with care is an act of love."
>
> —CRAIG CLAIBORNE, *The New York Times Cookbook*

1 Start your practice *before* you start grabbing supplies out of the refrigerator or cabinet. Form an image in your mind of the meal you will be preparing. Envision both the completed meal and the individual ingredients. Notice your intentions in preparing this meal.

2 As you begin gathering the things you will need, tune in to the body. Feel the body moving across the kitchen and reaching for each item. To help cultivate mindfulness, make an effort to move more slowly than you normally do.

3 As you chop, stir, and prepare, focus on one thing at a time. When turning on the stove, don't just turn the stove on. Feel the experience with your complete awareness. Whatever you are doing, bring your attention wholly to the task in front of you.

4 Use your senses. Notice if you're hearing, feeling in the body, tasting, smelling, or seeing. When you see water boiling, investigate the sight, the feeling of heat, and the sound. As you chop vegetables, listen to the noise of the knife, feel the utensil in your hand, and notice if you can smell anything. Using all five senses helps you remain present and interested.

5 When the meal is complete, pause to appreciate the experience. Recognize the effort you have put in. Bring gratitude to the energy that went into bringing the food to your kitchen in the first place. If you're feeding others, reflect that you are providing sustenance to these loved ones. Allow yourself to feel grateful.

30

Mindful Speech

Humans are social creatures. Rarely does a day go by where you don't interact with *anyone*—maybe you have a family, live with a roommate, or engage with people during work hours. When you talk, you can bring mindfulness to what you are saying, how it may impact others, and what your intentions are. This exercise takes just a few minutes, and you can utilize it anytime. Do this once or twice a day while on the phone, talking with a loved one, or during any social interaction.

STEPS

1   Before speaking, bring mindfulness to your intentions. Ask yourself why you are going to say whatever you plan on saying. Examine the possibility of saying it with even more kindness or patience.

2   Consider whether your words are timely and useful in this moment. We often gossip, interrupt, or talk simply to avoid uncomfortable silences. Think about whether or not this is the appropriate time to talk and what purpose your words will serve. ➤

75

3 If it's possible that your words will put somebody else down, interrupt a person currently speaking, or ring as untrue, try reconsidering your choice of words.

4 While talking, speak slowly and be mindful of the words you are using. When somebody responds either verbally or with body language, observe how it feels. Remember that you cannot control others, but you can bring mindfulness to your own responses.

5 When you are done talking, leave the words be. Listen to the other person and wait for the right time to talk again. As you practice mindful speech more regularly, you will be able to navigate challenging conversations with more ease.

RECOGNIZING UNWISE SPEECH: *You will likely notice times in which you speak without mindfulness. Set the goal to tune in to your habits of talking. If you find yourself gossiping a lot, create an intention to avoid gossip. If you interrupt others often, bring special awareness to this pattern. Don't beat yourself up. These are growing edges, and you have the opportunity to attend to them with compassion and kindness.*

31

Doing the Dishes

TIME: 10 MINUTES

On meditation retreats, I wash dozens of dishes silently every day. It took me years of silent retreats to appreciate this act as an opportunity to be mindful. For most of us, it seems like a dreaded chore. We wash the dishes in haste, rushing to get it done as quickly as possible. Instead, you can partake in this chore with present-time awareness and find some peace.

STEPS

1   Look at the dishes you are going to be cleaning. Notice any natural reactions you have to the task at hand. Try to bring to mind the meal that was consumed and how it supported the well-being and life of all those who ate.

2   Take a few deep breaths, centering your awareness in the body. Feel where you are standing and the weight pushing down the spine into the feet.

3   Begin to wash, one dish at a time. Stay focused on the dish directly in front of you in the moment. As you clean, tune in to the smells that arise of the soap and food. Watch the dishes become cleaner. Feel the warm water on your hands. Hear the sounds of the water and the scrubbing. ➤

4   Place the dish in your drying rack or dishwasher slowly, bringing awareness to the body as you do so.

5   Moving to the next dish, recognize that this is a new start. Let go of the dishes you have cleaned and the dishes still to be cleaned. Return to the one item you are cleaning right now.

6   Watch the mind wander. When it meanders, bring it back to the task at hand. You can always pause and take a few deep breaths to recenter yourself.

7   When you have cleaned the last dish, do not immediately stop the practice. Stay present as you wash your hands, clean up, and move on. With gratitude, recognize the reprieve you have been offered during this time.

32

Mindful Cleaning

TIME: 10 MINUTES

Like doing dishes, cleaning grants us the time to step back from our active days and rest in present-time awareness. Instead of focusing on the task itself or how you feel about it (most of us are usually not that excited to clean the house), use this time as a chance to take care of yourself and encourage the habit of mindfulness.

In this exercise, we will use the activity of sweeping. However, you can practice mindful cleaning while dusting, mopping, wiping down a counter, or doing any other household chore.

STEPS

1   Start your practice when you are gathering your cleaning supplies. Walking to get the broom, feel the feet moving across the floor. Pay attention to the feeling of moving through space toward your supplies.

2   Picking up the broom, bring awareness to the sense of touch. If the mind begins wandering into the future and the task at hand, bring yourself back to the body in the present moment. ➤

3 Sweeping is often repetitive, which can lead to a sense of boredom. To help stay in the present moment, try using a mantra. You can use a simple noting phrase, like "Left, right," or a phrase of loving-kindness, such as "May I live with ease." With each movement of the broom, mentally repeat the phrase in unison with the action.

4 Recognize any mental states that arise. If you are frustrated, notice that you are frustrated. If curiosity arises about some dirt, recognize that you are curious.

5 Continuing to clean, remember to check in with the body and state of mind. Notice the movements, the repetition, and the emotions that arise. Return to your mantra or phrase as many times as necessary.

6 When you are finished cleaning, stand still and take a deep breath. Observe the space you have cleaned, and recognize its representation of your clean mind!

33

Journaling

A regular journaling practice is a lovely way to check in with yourself. Dedicate a few minutes each day to examining your experience through writing. This exercise is best to do in the morning and at night in order to start and end your day with mindfulness. It also is useful to have a dedicated journal or notebook for this practice.

STEPS

1   Set aside five minutes in the morning to sit down and journal. As you sit down to do this exercise, tune in to the body sitting in the chair. Feel yourself sitting, the feet on the floor, and the pen or pencil in the hand.

2   Take a few deep breaths, grounding yourself in the present moment. Recognize the state of the mind this morning. Is it calm, anxious, fearful, or hopeful? You don't need to fix anything; just notice where the mind is today. ➤

3 For a few minutes, mindfully write about your current experience and the day ahead. You may set a timer if this feels like a daunting task. Address how you feel this morning, your state of mind, and any intentions you have for the day. Ask yourself if you have any worries, hopes, or events on the mind.

4 Finishing your journaling practice, return to the breath for a few moments before moving on with your day.

5 At night, return to this practice. For five minutes, reflect on your day. Identify anything you are grateful for, reflect on things that you could have handled better, and note any points of mindfulness during your day.

THE MEDITATION JOURNAL

You can also incorporate journaling into your meditation practice. After you sit in traditional meditation, open your journal and put down your experience in writing. Note whether the mind was focused or wandering, how it felt to practice, and anything unique or interesting about that day's practice. Writing about your practice provides extra space for you to look at your experience with curiosity and equanimity.

34

The Moving World

TIME: 10 MINUTES

The very nature of mindfulness is to tune in to your experience at any given moment, noticing as you go that *every* experience is impermanent. That is to say, everything is always changing. Feelings come and go, thoughts arise and pass, and sounds pop up and disappear. We can use this changing nature as the object of our awareness during the day. Tuning in to all the change in the world will help you identify impermanence in action and give you a variety of things to focus on.

STEPS

1   Sit outside or near a window, and leave the eyes open. Set the intention to rest in awareness of your present-time experience. Place the awareness on the body and the breath, taking in where you are and how you are sitting.

2   Begin by noticing where you can feel motion in the body as you sit still. Rest with the breath and pay attention to the abdomen, chest, shoulders, and anywhere else you can sense the change. ➤

3 Open to your sense of hearing. Notice the presence of any noises, specifically tuning in to their changing nature. You may hear cars coming and going, your breath flowing in and out, birds chirping and stopping, or any other sounds as they rise and eventually fade away. When a sound comes into your awareness, focus on it for a few moments before opening up to other sounds again.

4 Finally, use your sense of sight and see the movement in the world. What can you see that is moving or changing? There may be obvious movement, like cars driving, trees blowing in the wind, or people on the move. You may also notice subtle signs of movement and change, like the browning leaves of autumn, clouds floating across the sky, or a pothole that has been growing.

5 After 10 minutes, return to the sensations of movement in the body. Reground yourself for a few moments before returning to your day.

35

Color Your World

The world is full of different colors, and you can practice mindfulness by paying attention to which ones you are seeing in the present moment. Seeing is a different experience from tuning in to the breath or body, but it offers the same opportunity to be deeply present. We rely heavily on our sense of sight, making it a powerful tool for the cultivation of mindfulness.

STEPS

1   You can do this practice anywhere. You may be sitting at your desk, taking a ride on the bus, or walking down the street. Wherever you decide to do this practice, set aside 10 minutes to dedicate yourself to it.

2   Arrive in the present moment. Take a few mindful breaths, feel the body where it is, and allow your energy to settle.

3   Pick one color to focus on. You may try starting with red one day, and work your way through the traditional rainbow spectrum on each subsequent day. ➤

4 Find one thing you can see that is the color you have picked. Look at it with beginner's mind, as if you have never seen this thing before. Note what it is and its size and shape.

5 After a few moments, look for something else that is this color. Observe this object in the same way.

6 Continuing with this practice, notice when your mind wanders off. You can always return to the sensation of breathing, using the breath as the anchor for your awareness. You may find it helpful to mentally note exactly what you are seeing. For example, a red stop sign doesn't get labeled "red stop sign"; it becomes "red, octagon, writing, metal."

7 When 10 minutes have passed, allow the eyes to close for a moment. Take a few deep breaths, let go of the practice, and return to your daily life.

A DAY OF COLORING: *You can modify this practice a bit to incorporate it throughout your day. Pick a color and use it as an awareness trigger (see Exercise 26, The Awareness Trigger, page 67). Keep this color in mind throughout your day, and just notice whenever you see it. This practice can remind you to stay present during your day or to return to mindfulness as you get caught up in your day-to-day activities.*

36

Dedicated Listening

TIME: 10 MINUTES

This exercise requires a partner. Ask a friend or loved one to join you for 10 minutes of practice. They may be a complete beginner to mindfulness or have a practice of their own. It doesn't matter!

In this exercise, you both will be working with the practice of listening mindfully. Whomever you choose, they should be somebody you trust. The practice will require some vulnerability.

The partner who is listening should listen attentively, with a clear mind and no judgment. Try to be present with the experience of listening, and let go of the need to respond. While listening, you should retain awareness of your own experience as you take in the words the other is saying. Explore what it means to be present while listening.

When speaking, practice mindful speech. Be honest, allow yourself to be vulnerable, and observe the words you are saying.

1   Sit down at eye level with your partner. Choose one person to speak first while the other listens.

2   Set a timer for four minutes. The person who speaks first can begin talking about goals and intentions they have—for their day, for their loved ones, for their future, and so on.

3   When the timer goes off, switch roles. The other person can now talk about their goals and intentions, while the other person practices mindful listening.

4   When the timer completes, spend a few minutes conversing. How was the practice? What was it like to sit and just listen? Was it difficult to not respond?

PROMPTS: *You can change the topics you speak about as you see fit. Instead of talking about intentions, you can discuss fears, happy memories, how your week is going, or anything else. You can use this practice to examine different parts of your life and to learn to be fully present while listening.*

37

Mindful Bathing

TIME: 15 MINUTES

Showering and bathing are common times to check out. You let your mind wander, go completely into autopilot, or just shut down mentally. Instead, you can use this time to work on your mindfulness practice. Make your shower time a cleansing ritual for the body *and* the mind, using the prompts in this exercise. You can practice with any or all of your senses in the shower, but for this practice, you will focus primarily on the physical body.

STEPS

1 Begin your practice before turning on the water. Stand for a moment and bring your awareness to the rising and falling of the breath in the chest. Feel the lungs expand and contract with each inhalation and exhalation.

2 As you turn on the water, feel your hands on the knob, watch the water begin to flow, and hear the noise of the shower. Notice if heat or steam fills the room.

3 Once you step into the shower, acknowledge what you are feeling. You may notice the temperature change, the sensation of water on the skin, and any response of the body to the water. ➤

4 Go through your usual routine, feeling the movement, texture, and points of contact in the body. Rest your attention on the hands and skin as you wash and rinse your body. Moving more slowly than you normally do will help the mind stay present.

5 Wrapping up the showering process, don't let your awareness go. Stay present as you shut the water off and get out. Feel the towel on your skin as you dry yourself. Moving on with your day, try to retain this awareness of the body.

38

I Like . . .

One of the most pleasant ways to cultivate mindfulness is to notice the things that bring you joy. By taking the time to appreciate these moments, you are training the mind to recognize more of them in the future. In this practice, you will be taking a short walk and noticing what makes you happy.

"Joy does not simply happen to us. You have to choose joy and keep choosing it every day."

—HENRI NOUWEN, *The Inner Voice of Love:*
A Journey through Anguish to Freedom

1   Find somewhere to walk. It may be in a park, on a trail, or around your block. You do not need to be anywhere special.

2   Before starting to walk, stand and take a few deep breaths. Notice the feeling of breathing at your nostrils. Ground yourself in the sensation of your feet on the ground, tuning in to the weight of the body and the gravity holding you down.

3   Begin walking at a normal pace. While moving, look for something you like. You may not *love* everything you see or experience, but there are likely sights, feelings, and sounds that you like. It can be as simple as a color or a shape of a thing (not even the actual thing itself).

4   When you notice something you like, say to yourself, "I like that tree," or "I like the color blue," or "I like the birds chirping." Say this silently in your head whenever you notice something you enjoy. Or you can say it out loud if you want!

5   Remember, there is no right or wrong with this practice. Be true to yourself and whatever you like. When the mind wanders off or falls into judgment, come back to the present moment by grounding yourself in the feeling of the feet on the ground as you walk. Then open back up to the experiences you are enjoying.

6   After 15 minutes or so have passed, you can return to your day. Make some effort to bring this practice with you into your life. Whenever you notice something you enjoy—however subtle it may be—note to yourself that you like it.

39

Where Are the Feet?

TIME: 5 MINUTES

This practice comes from my training with trauma therapists. In trauma therapy, the client is often encouraged to bring awareness to the feet. This is a grounding practice that helps engage the parasympathetic nervous system, which is responsible for calming the mind and body.

STEPS

1   Consider how you are going to remind yourself to feel your feet throughout your day. You can put a sticky note on your computer, set a reminder on your phone, or use one of the other awareness triggers you have discovered. If you use a reminder or sticky note, write the simple question, "Where are my feet?"

2   During your day, bring your awareness to the feet. Feel how they are resting. Scan the foot from the heel to the arch, ball, toe, and top of each foot. ➤

3 Take a few deep breaths as you continue to pay attention to the feet. Allow the body and mind to settle a bit. With each exhalation, allow the feet to relax.

4 Continuing with your day, be ready for the reminder to pop up again. Each time, return to this brief practice of relaxing into the grounding sensations within the feet.

40

Shopping Mindfully

TIME: 15 MINUTES

Going to the grocery store can send us into a state of anxiety and impatience rather quickly. All the decisions to make, the crowds of people, and the details of our shopping lists create the perfect conditions to "check out." But within the busyness of shopping, this activity also provides an effective environment for mindfulness practice.

STEPS

1   Before going inside, slow down to connect with your intention to shop mindfully. Breathing deeply, allow the body to relax with each exhale. Let the shoulders drop down, relax the abdomen, and release any tension in the jaw.

2   As you walk up to the doors, practice a few moments of walking meditation. Feel each foot as it lifts off the ground and is placed down in front of you. Just for the moment, let go of the thoughts in the thinking mind, and relax your awareness down into the feet. ➤

3 Once inside, spend a brief minute taking it all in. Check in with the six sense-doors of mindfulness: seeing, hearing, smelling, tasting, feeling in the body, and thinking. Note the colors and lights, any smells in the air, how the body is standing, the noise of the grocery store, and your state of mind. There isn't a right or wrong answer; just tune in to your personal experience.

4 As you move toward a section of the store to begin your shopping, stay present with the body. Feel the feet on the ground and the muscles in the legs working to keep you moving.

5 When you pick something up to place in your cart or basket, stay in touch with the sensations in the body. Feel the arm and hand reach. As you grab the item, feel the texture, temperature, and weight. Setting it in your cart, pay attention to how it feels to release the object.

6 Continue shopping with this mindfulness of the body. Each item offers an opportunity to practice, as does the space between grabbing things. When it is time to check out (from the grocery store, not from your mind), wait in line mindfully. See Exercise 45, What Are You Waiting For? (page 105), for a mindful waiting practice.

ADDING NEW SENSES: *If you find the mind wandering a lot while shopping, try focusing on one of your senses. Instead of noting simply what is present in the body, tune in to the colors you see or the sounds you hear. When you see the color red, note that you're seeing red. When you hear someone talking, note that you're hearing someone talking. This can give the mind some extra stimuli to help it stay present.*

41

Stop and Smell the Roses

TIME: 15 MINUTES

Many of the practices in this book focus on the senses of feeling, hearing, and thinking. But your sense of smell is an especially powerful connection to your mind. When you smell something, a signal is sent directly into the neocortex and limbic system, making it a powerful trigger for inducing memories, emotions, and thoughts. This practice will give you a framework for investigating the sense of smell more deeply in your life.

STEPS

1   Find a place to walk where you can spend 15 minutes outside. It may be in a park, around your neighborhood, or out on a trail.

2   Begin with a moment to ground yourself in the present. Focus on mindfulness of the external world. Rather than focusing on the body, open your eyes, listen to the sounds, and recognize where you are.

3   Begin walking mindfully. It can be helpful to walk slower than you normally do. Stay in tune with the world around you. ➤

4   When you see something natural that may have a scent, pause and smell it. It may be a flower, an herb, a plant, or the smell of the ground after the rain. As you are smelling, close the eyes and bring your full awareness to the aroma. Immerse yourself in the experience by making the sense of smell the sole focus of your attention.

5   After a few moments of this, leave it be and continue walking. When you come across another aromatic object, stop and smell it with presence. Stay curious and open. This practice is different from working with other senses, because you have to intentionally smell something rather than just observe.

6   When you are done with your walk, try to remember this practice throughout the day. Whether you're eating a meal, drinking tea, or driving home, tune in to the smells that come and go. Observe your reactions to these, as we often have strong positive or negative reactions to scents.

42

Bedtime Mindfulness

TIME: 10 MINUTES

You may have woven mindfulness practice into your day—but as soon as you lie down in bed, you notice the mind beginning to race. As you settle down for the evening, the mind may not always read the situation accurately. With the stimuli of daily life over, the mind can seem louder than usual. This exercise can be used in these moments to help settle the mind and body as you prepare for sleep.

STEPS

1   Standing next to your bed, take a few deep breaths. Center yourself in the present moment, bringing your awareness to the body as it is right now.

2   When you climb into bed, remain aware of what is occurring in the body. As you lie down, feel the body assume a resting position. ➤

3 Use the breath to bring mindfulness to the body and cultivate relaxation. As you breathe in, feel the lungs fill with air. When you exhale, feel the body soften into your mattress. Picture yourself falling deeper into the mattress as the body relaxes with each exhale.

4 Start a body scan at the top of the head, moving down the body to the toes. As your attention rests on each part, relax it and soften into the bed with every exhale.

5 When you reach your toes, return to the body as a whole and the practice of breathing deeply. Continue softening.

43

Accentuate the Positive

TIME: 5 MINUTES

Dr. Rick Hanson, the esteemed psychologist and mindfulness teacher, points out that the brain has a negativity bias. The mind naturally clings to unpleasant experiences in order to "brace" you and protect you from danger. By actively seeking out moments of joy, you encourage the brain to shift that bias. As the saying goes, what you put your attention on grows—if you look for pleasant experiences, you will find them.

In this exercise, you will work to bring intentional mindfulness to the positive moments of your day.

STEPS

1 Start your day with the intention of finding good things; be a hunter on the lookout for something that brings you happiness.

2 When you notice anything that makes you happy—whether it's making it through a green light or calling an old friend—fully take in the moment. First, notice your mental state. Try to identify what the experience is in the mind: calmness, relaxation, contentment, satisfaction, and so on. ➤

3   Next, bring your awareness to the body. Focus on the chest, abdomen, and shoulders. Notice any feelings of ease in the body, openness, or relief from tension. As you breathe, make space to feel the happiness all over.

4   Without clinging to the feeling, try to stay in tune with the experience. Let the feelings fade naturally and notice when they have left.

5   Remain open during your day to other joys you may experience. Remember, they do not have to be grand moments of elation. You can use the subtle moments of contentment and ease.

44

People Are People

TIME: 5 MINUTES

Mindfulness is not just a quality you bring to your own body and mind; it's also possible to tune in to those around us with mindfulness. This is called *external mindfulness*, and it is an important part of practice. When you see another person, do you see them as a three-dimensional being? Or do you label them as "checkout clerk," "soccer mom," or "annoying coworker"? With practice, you can train the mind to objectively see other people as humans— just like you.

STEPS

1 Engage in this exercise when you are in the presence of other people. You can spend a few minutes with this practice at work, in the grocery store, or sitting on a park bench. It works best to start with people you don't know that much about, so I recommend a public place. As you practice, take it up a notch by applying this to your loved ones. ➤

2   When you see someone else, notice the label the mind habitually gives that person. Notice if you find the person attractive, what their job or role is, or any other snap judgments. Don't force anything down or deny the presence of these thoughts—your mind is designed to categorize and label things, and we *all* judge other people. Just notice whatever is present.

3   Begin to observe this person with beginner's mind, as if you've never seen a person before. Start to see them as a living, breathing, and feeling being. Recognize that this person has friends, a job, a place they need to be in five minutes, and so on. This person loves people and has people who love them.

4   Bring awareness to this person's possible experience. Like you, they have hopes, dreams, fears, sorrows, regrets, and joy. You don't need to know this person's whole life story to be sure that they are subject to pleasant and unpleasant emotional experiences.

5   End your practice with this person by offering a single phrase of loving-kindness, such as "May you be happy today."

6   You can continue this practice with other people you run into during your day. Take just a few moments to reflect, recognize, and offer a phrase of loving-kindness.

45

What Are You Waiting For?

TIME: 10 MINUTES

Waiting is an unavoidable fact of life. Often when we're waiting— in traffic, at the DMV, for our food to arrive—we grow impatient or frustrated. We focus entirely on getting to the front of the line and completing the task.

In these moments when you have nothing to do but wait, you have a perfect opportunity to practice and encourage mindfulness.

STEPS

1 Begin this practice whenever you are waiting during your day. Whether you're physically waiting in line or waiting on hold on the telephone, use the experience of waiting as your cue to practice.

2 Pay attention to what it is you are waiting for. You are likely waiting for something specific. Bring this to mind, recognizing the nature of the experience. ➤

105

3 Check in to see if there is any impatience or frustration present with the waiting. Watch for the energy in the body that results in fidgeting or the urge to take your cell phone out of your pocket. If you feel the energy of impatience, soften into it and allow it to be present.

4 Feel the feet flat on the floor. Gently scan the body from the ground up, bringing awareness to each part of the body for one breath. Use the body scan to stay present, noticing any difficulties that arise.

5 When you move forward in line or get to the end, continue practicing mindfulness of the body. Notice if the body relaxes or gets excited when you get toward the front of the line. See how the body feels when you finish the task and have the waiting behind you.

46

Stealth Kindness

TIME: 15 MINUTES

This practice was first introduced to me on a daylong retreat in Los Angeles. As our group meditated in the middle of the city, the teacher explained this as a way to bring our practice to the real world. Although this is a practice in cultivating loving-kindness, it can also help you let go of overthinking and concentrate the mind.

STEPS

1 You can do this practice while walking, driving, or sitting in a space wherever other people are present. This can be a part of your normal routine, or you can set aside special time for it.

2 Pick one person at a time, whoever grabs your attention naturally. Recognize that this is a person with hopes, dreams, fears, regrets, memories, and loved ones. Just like you, this person wants to be happy. Offer a simple phrase of loving-kindness in your head, such as "May you live with ease today." ➤

3 Move to the next person you see and repeat. Allow yourself to enjoy the practice of dropping "kindness bombs" on the other people you see.

4 Continue doing this for several minutes. If you run out of people, you can return to someone you have already visited. Or you can offer yourself a little kindness.

5 When you get to where you are going or are ready to move on with your day, let the loving-kindness phrases go. However, don't hesitate to return to them at any point as a reminder of your intention to be kind.

47

Mindful Media

TIME: 20 MINUTES

Just as you take food into your body, consuming both healthy and not-so-healthy options, you also consume media throughout the day. You listen to music, watch TV, read the news, and so on. Although these may provide knowledge and entertainment, they can also create anxiety and stress in our minds and bodies or take us away from our connection to the mind.

This exercise offers a few different ways to bring mindfulness to these moments of consumption. They don't necessarily need to be done step-by-step.

STEPS

1   First, consider what the impact may be of what you are choosing to consume. Are you reading the news to inform yourself, or to fuel frustration? Perhaps the television show you watch has quite a bit of violence and gets your nervous system going. This isn't to label a show, story, or song as good or bad. It's merely about recognizing the effects of your choice. ➤

2   As you consume the piece of media, notice the response of the mind
    and body. If you are watching TV, mute the volume during commercials
    to check in with yourself. When reading a news story, pause every few
    paragraphs. Watch for stress, anxiety, or increased energy in the body.

3   Whether you're watching television, reading news, or listening to music,
    try to be fully present with your experience. Watch the individuals on the
    TV, pay attention to the details of the news story, and hear the individual
    instruments of a song. Dive into the experience with your full attention.

RUINING CONSUMPTION

You may feel as if this practice ruins the experience of
consuming—most of us watch TV, for example, as a means
of checking *out*, not *in*. As you begin to pick apart your
choices, they may become less entertaining in the traditional
sense. This is normal, and it's a part of practice. See if you can
still bring appreciation and an easygoing attitude to these
experiences, and try not to take it too seriously. Notice joy,
laughter, and any other positive reactions you have to what
you're consuming.

48

Driving with Mindfulness

TIME: 10 MINUTES

Driving can be a time of stress, autopilot, or downright rage. But similar to mindful bathing, it's a prime opportunity to cultivate mindfulness, partly because it's a natural transition between one part of your day and another.

If you're the one driving, remember that safety is the number one priority! You may try this practice in a parking lot first, in a quiet neighborhood, or in a place where you feel totally comfortable behind the wheel. Mindful driving can also help you be less distracted while driving, making you a better driver.

STEPS

1   Start this practice before you actually begin driving. Sitting in your car, feel the points of contact. Tune in to the feet on the pedals, the sensation of sitting in the seat, and the hands on the wheel. As you turn your car on, feel and hear the sensation of the car starting. ➤

2 As you begin moving, pay attention to the experience of driving. You don't need to do anything special. Just watch your experience with present-time awareness. Notice other cars, the noises of driving, and anything else that arises.

3 Try using a simple noting practice. When you hear your blinker, note "Blinker" in your head. When you turn, note "Turning." Notice any movement, sounds, sights, or feelings in the body as you drive.

4 If and when you see another driver, try offering a phrase of loving-kindness. Say to the person, "May you drive with ease."

49

Killing Time

TIME: 10 MINUTES

No matter how busy you are, there are always some moments when you just need to "kill some time." You may scroll through social media, play a game on your phone, or read the news. When you have a few minutes to kill, you can use it as a period of practice. Instead of telling yourself that these habits are bad or wrong, you can use them as a focus for your mindfulness, thus making them more restorative and restful.

You can use this exercise to take a break from your day at work or at home, using your few free minutes to arrive in the present moment. This exercise will focus specifically on the use of smartphones, as this is a common way many of us check out during the day.

STEPS

1   When you have a few minutes to spare in which you would normally kill time, notice the habitual urge to *waste* time. (This doesn't mean you label the habit wrong or bad; it's just about observing.) ➤

2   As you begin participating in your normal method of killing time, bring
    some mindfulness to the act. If you take your phone out, pay attention
    to your state of mind as you do so. Can you be fully present as you begin
    scrolling through social media, playing a game, or reading a news story?

3   Use the sense of sight as the object of your awareness. Watch what you
    are doing as you do it. Pay attention to the picture as a whole, and the
    individual parts of what you are seeing. Notice colors, shapes, movement,
    and anything that grabs your attention.

4   As you click the screen or interact with your phone, be mindful of the
    interaction between the body and the device.

5   Continue to "kill time" mindfully, attending to the actions with a gentle
    awareness. Don't judge yourself for taking a break. Be proud you are using
    your break to take care of yourself and cultivate mindfulness.

50

Stilling the Mind

TIME: 10 MINUTES

As you go about your day, you may notice that your practice gets further and further away from your awareness. The mind goes on autopilot for hours on end. This can sometimes result in feelings of anxiety or rapid thinking.

You can always use this practice of stilling the mind to help settle yourself back into calm awareness. When you're focused and relaxed, you are more productive and able to better attend to your experience.

STEPS

1   Stop what you are doing to set aside 10 minutes to practice. Notice how this feels in the mind. If thoughts about chores, tasks, or the future arise, just notice that they are present.

2   Utilize the breath to help relax the body. As you inhale, invite in relaxation. With the exhale, allow the muscles in the body to relax. ➤

3 Recognize that although the mind may not always do what you want it to, it is the mind that allows you to experience joy, pleasure, and gratitude. Begin offering the mind a few phrases of loving-kindness with the intention of building a gentler relationship with its thoughts. You can use the phrases "May my mind be at ease" and "May I be at ease with my mind."

4 Continue repeating these phrases, directing them toward the mind. Use the phrases in your head as the object of your awareness. Try to hear the words in your head and connect with the meaning of the phrase.

5 When you notice the mind is agitated, anxious, or overactive, use a one-word note. Note "Thinking," "Anxious," or whatever is present for you. Then, return to your phrases.

6 Continue with the repetition of phrases until time is up. Remember to be gentle, not forcing or straining to concentrate. If the mind wanders off, just notice it is doing so and gently bring it back.

CARRYING THE STILL MIND WITH YOU: *You can bring this practice with you as you transition back into your day. During your day, notice the moments in which the mind is especially active or agitated. Use that as an awareness trigger to pause for a brief moment, notice the thoughts you are experiencing, and offer the mind a wish of ease. You can do this a couple of times and then return to whatever you were doing. This helps you retrain the mind to respond with friendliness and awareness, rather than falling victim to whatever thoughts are arising.*

PART THREE

Mindful Moods

Difficult, painful, or challenging experiences often take us out of mindfulness, and we all experience anxiety, frustration, sadness, and anger. In these moments, you have an opportunity to respond however you choose. By tending to your painful emotions with mindfulness, you learn new ways to work with them instead of pushing them away or fighting them. Over time, you'll grow less reactive and better able to meet the hard times with care and awareness.

The exercises in this part offer various techniques and tools to help you approach the tough days with awareness, compassion, and softness.

51

Calming the Body

TIME: 15 MINUTES

When the mind grows agitated, the body often follows suit. Luckily, the relationship between mind and body is a two-way street. As you calm the body, the mind will likewise relax.

I learned this practice in my month meditating with Thanissaro Bhikkhu, a senior monk in the Thai Forest Tradition of Theravada Buddhism. It is a powerful way to encourage the body to relax, and anyone can do it.

STEPS

1   Pick a position in which to do this exercise. You can do this exercise sitting, standing, or lying down. It can be done anywhere or anytime you need to calm down.

2   Allow the eyes to close. Tune in to the sensation of breathing at the nostrils. It may help to take some deep breaths to arrive into your present-time experience. ➤

3   Begin with the left arm. As you breathe in, picture the arm filling with the energy of the breath. As you breathe out, imagine pushing the breath energy out through your fingertips. Tune in to the left arm as you do this, keeping both the physical body and the visualization in your awareness. When the mind wanders off into thought, gently bring it back to the breath.

4   After two or three minutes, switch to the right arm. Breathe in, filling the arm with the breath energy. Exhale and release the energy through the right fingertips. Continue with the right arm for a few minutes.

5   Now, shift your awareness to the torso. Visualize filling the entire chest and abdomen with breath energy as you inhale. Push the breath down, out through the bottom of the spine and tailbone, as you exhale.

6   After a few minutes, continue with each of the legs. Start with the left leg for a couple of minutes, pushing the breath out through the foot. Switch to the right leg, continuing the same practice for two or three more minutes.

7   At the end, try to bring it all together. Breathe in and fill your entire body with the breath. Imagine the body being filled with the energy of the breath from head to toe. Exhaling, let the breath out through the fingertips, the base of the spine, and the feet.

52

Dealing with Negativity

TIME: 10 MINUTES

No matter how much you try to think positive thoughts and be optimistic about the future, unpleasant thoughts will still arise. You cannot avoid them, and there is no use in pretending they aren't present. Your mindfulness practice can help you approach these thoughts with curiosity. As you build an understanding of your unpleasant thinking patterns, they will no longer hook you in so strongly. You can learn to allow them to be present without letting them consume you.

This exercise is a practice in letting thoughts go so that you are better able to do it when negative thoughts arise.

STEPS

1   Close the eyes and tune in to the points of contact in the body. Feel yourself grounded and stable as you sit. Breathe deeply, feeling the body supported by the chair or cushion. ➤

2　Pay attention to the experience in your mind. Notice any thoughts as they arise, and try to identify any emotions that go with them. Pay special attention to negative thoughts, and note what you're feeling or thinking. Try to avoid the word *negative*, and instead identify each thought as sad, unpleasant, irritating, painful, or otherwise.

3　Continue for five minutes, noting any thoughts and their accompanying feelings.

4　Make *impermanence* the focus of this practice. See each thought and acknowledge it as it passes. Continue to note what you're thinking about and how it feels, using noting phrases like "Coming, going" or "Arising, passing," if you choose.

5　After five minutes, return to the body for a few deep breaths. Remind yourself that thoughts come and go, and you have a choice in whether or not you believe each one.

LETTING GO OF JUDGMENT: *You may notice the title of this exercise includes the word* negativity, *but the practice itself can include any thoughts, regardless of their tone. When you identify thoughts as negative, you immediately invite judgment and resistance to them. Instead, try noticing the feeling tone of each thought, which is often unpleasant. This can help discourage judgments from arising about the mind.*

53

Stopping Rumination

TIME: 15 MINUTES

Rumination is a powerful form of deluded thinking. You think about the past obsessively, despite the fact that you cannot change what happened. You stew in your resentments, replay conversations, beat yourself up, and relive an event over and over. It happens to all of us, and it can be quite painful. Mindfulness practice helps you see those patterns clearly, respond to them with patient understanding, and begin to detach yourself from their power.

Ruminating often shows up as "background noise"—a constant stream of obsessive negativity shadowing you throughout the day. This practice will help you call that inner voice into the light, dissect it, and, hopefully, diffuse some of its hold over you.

STEPS

1 Close the eyes and allow the body to relax. Use the breath to help encourage ease in the body. With each exhale, soften the muscles of the body a bit more. You may bring special attention to the abdomen, shoulders, and jaw. ➤

2   Look at the thoughts going through the mind. If you have been ruminating about something specific, acknowledge the event or situation about which you are thinking.

3   Turn this over in the mind, examining it from a place of curiosity and interest.

4   Begin cultivating equanimity, the state of balance and nonattachment in the midst of charged emotions. Ask yourself if you are able to change this situation in the past. Offer some phrases of equanimity and compassion:

> *I cannot change the past.*
>
> *May I be at ease with the mind.*
>
> *May I care about this difficulty.*

5   After a few minutes of this, turn your attention toward the present. Although you cannot control the past, you do have power over your actions right now. Replace the rumination with the recognition that you can choose to act in ways that encourage happiness. Offer these phrases silently in your head:

> *May I act with wisdom.*
>
> *May I respond with compassion.*
>
> *May I move forward.*

6   Continue the phrases for five minutes or so. When the rumination recurs, return to the phrases and your intention to move forward.

7   Finishing your period of practice, carry these phrases with you. Whenever the mind falls into the pattern of thinking about the past, offer a phrase of equanimity or wise action.

54

Releasing the Pressure Valve

TIME: 10 MINUTES

Some emotions carry an especially strong energy. The mind becomes highly active, and the body grows tense. This often happens when you are angry, anxious, or overwhelmed. In these moments, you can benefit from "letting off some steam." You can use this exercise to relieve pressure in the moment and bring some softness to your experience.

STEPS

1   Begin by closing the eyes and tuning in to the breath. Fill the chest completely and empty it smoothly and slowly. Take a few deep breaths like this, resting your attention on the rise and fall of the chest.

2   Recognize what you are feeling. In an effort to not own it completely or allow it to consume you, try to give it a name that evokes a little love. For example, if you're feeling angry, you may notice that "Angry Buddha" is present. Or you can give it a name like "Little Johnny." This will help you separate yourself from the emotion while also encouraging you to deal with it from a place of sweetness. ➤

3 See if you can find a location in the body where the emotion is present. You may feel tightness in the chest, a pit in the stomach, or tension in the shoulders. Instead of trying to rid yourself of that feeling, make space for it. Picture the emotion as a dense ball in this spot and allow it to spread out and make its way through the entire body. Keep some awareness on the breath to help stabilize you during this practice.

4 Finally, breathe in the essence of the emotion, and exhale its energy out. You may picture yourself allowing the emotion to gently dissipate as you breathe. Don't try to push the feelings away; rather, gently allow them to continue on. You may even try saying goodbye to Angry Buddha or Little Johnny.

55

What Is This Emotion?

TIME: 10 MINUTES

This exercise is an adaptation of some of the body-scanning practices in this book as well as the emotion-based exercises above. It is especially useful when you feel overwhelmed by emotion and unable to articulate what's going on.

You will need a pen and paper or a journal for this exercise.

STEPS

1   Set aside 10 minutes for this practice. You can use this practice anytime during your day, but it is especially useful when you notice a strong emotion present. You might be experiencing anxiety and stress, or something pleasant, like joy or gratitude.

2   With the eyes open, drop your awareness into the body. Acknowledge the points in the body where you can feel this emotion. For example, many people experience anxiety in the chest, stomach, and limbs. Anger or fear often arises in the stomach, causes tension in the shoulders, and results in a scrunched brow. ➤

3   Recognizing the emotional experience in the body, write what you feel. Jot down where you are feeling something and what it feels like. Continue alternating between observing the body and writing your observations down. Be as specific as you can.

4   When you have covered the experience in the body, turn your awareness toward the mind. Look for both individual thoughts and overall mental states. A mental state may be something like anxiety, hope, or the craving to fix something. The individual thoughts may be about a person, an event, or a problem that needs solving. Again, write these down as you notice them.

5   Finally, allow the eyes to close for a minute or two. Tune in to the sense of sight with closed eyes. Notice if the sight feels dark or light, if there is movement, or if the mind is visualizing something. There isn't a correct answer. As you open the eyes and write your experience on paper, let go of any judgment.

6   Read what you have written carefully and slowly. When you finish, see if you feel more clarity around your emotions.

CRAVING AND AVERSION

The mind habitually craves pleasant experiences and averts itself from unpleasant ones. In mindfulness practice, craving and aversion are seen as the two main causes of suffering. Notice when you find yourself craving more pleasant experiences or pushing away the unpleasant ones. You don't need to change or fix anything. Notice when the mind falls into liking and disliking experiences or feelings, and include this in your notes as you write about your experience.

56

Cooling the Fire

TIME: 15 MINUTES

Anger is an emotion that may consume you completely, causing you to act in ways that are harmful or unproductive. When anger arises, the mind can fall victim to harsh thoughts, judgments, and obsessions. By creating space and responding to your anger with compassionate awareness, you can build resiliency and adjust your anger response. This exercise offers a way to deal with anger when you're right in the midst of it.

STEPS

1   When you notice anger, frustration, or irritation rising, allow the eyes to close. Know that you are feeling anger. Do not try to rid yourself of it, talk yourself out of it, or pretend it is not there.

2   Breathe deeply into the abdomen. Feel the chest and stomach fill with air and exhale slowly. When you exhale, make an effort to really empty the lungs. Breathe deeply for the first few minutes.

3   Bring to mind the situation that is causing anger. When you are new to this practice, it is helpful to work with something that is mildly frustrating, as the feeling of full-on rage may be too overwhelming. ➤

4 As you tune in to the rising anger in the mind, allow yourself to feel what is happening in the body. Notice the sensations that indicate anger. You may feel tension in the shoulders, shallow breathing, a pit in the stomach, or a number of other changes in the body.

5 Tend to each experience in the body with a compassionate awareness. Recognize the tension by noting "Tension" and staying with the experience for a few breaths. Then open your awareness and see what else is occurring in the body.

6 After 10 minutes of examining anger in the body, switch to awareness of the mind. Ask yourself what may be underneath the anger or causing it. There may be feelings of pain, betrayal, wanting to control something, or some perceived lack of safety. If you cannot find something at first, patiently wait to see if anything comes up.

7 When you do notice something underneath the anger, name it. If you find that you are hurt, note "Hurt." Respond with a phrase of compassion, such as "May I learn to care about this pain."

8 When you finish this practice, take a break to journal. Write what you noticed in the body, what you found underneath the anger, and how it felt to try to respond with compassion. As you continue to experience anger, you will find yourself able to see it with wisdom and patience.

57

Smiling

Mindfulness practice means feeling how you feel. Instead of avoiding or shoving down pain, you accept it with care and attention. But that doesn't mean you have to sit in pain, doing nothing. The simple practice of smiling can actually trigger joy in the mind and body, helping relieve some of this pain. In this exercise, you will mindfully tune in to how it feels to bring a gentle smile across the face.

"Sometimes your joy is the source of your smile, but sometimes your smile is the source of your joy."

—**THICH NHAT HANH**

1 Allow the eyes to close, and find a comfortable sitting posture. If you are able to, keep the spine straight to invite energy and alertness into the mind and body.

2 Begin by bringing your attention to the sensations of the body breathing. Start with the abdomen, tuning in to the rising and falling. Let the body breathe itself; you don't need to breathe in any certain way.

3 After two minutes, move your attention to the chest. Feel the expansion and contraction here as the body continues to breathe. When you notice that the mind has wandered, simply bring the chest back into your awareness. Allow two more minutes to pass.

4 Now move your attention up to the nostrils. You may feel the breath at the tip or base of the nose or on the upper lip. Pay attention to the subtle sensation of breathing here.

5 Open your awareness up slightly to scan the face. From the forehead down to the chin, notice what you can physically feel. Tune in to the eyes, the mouth, the jaw, the cheeks, and anything else that grabs your attention.

6 Finally, allow yourself to softly smile. You may try thinking of something that brings you joy as a form of encouragement. As you smile, notice how the face and the breath feel. Tune in to any changes in the breath, the muscles in the face, and any feelings that arise.

7 You may try letting the smile go and bringing it back several times, tuning in each time to the experience in the body as you do so.

8 When you complete the practice and allow the eyes to open, sustain the smile for a moment. Let the smile fade slowly on its own.

58

Finger Breathing

TIME: 5 MINUTES

This practice was introduced to me by my wife, Elizabeth. As an associate marriage and family therapist, she incorporates mindfulness into her work with teenagers and young adults. Although she uses this exercise with young people, I find it to be useful with people of all ages. This technique is excellent for grounding, centering, and calming the mind.

STEPS

1 Incorporate this practice whenever you wish for a few moments of mindfulness. You can be driving, sitting, standing, or walking.

2 Begin with the thumb at the base of the pinky finger on the same hand. With the inhale, gently move the thumb up to the tip of the pinky.

3 Pause briefly between the inhale and the exhale, and softly press the tips of the thumb and pinky together.

4 With the exhale, move the thumb gently back down the finger. ➤

5 Continue this practice with the other fingers. When you reach the index finger, move back down to the pinky.

6 You can do this as many times as you like. Use one hand or both hands, or alternate. As you move through the fingers and breathe, rest your awareness on the synchronization of the breath and the movement in the hands.

59

Extending the Exhale

TIME: 10 MINUTES

This exercise also comes from Elizabeth. The way the body breathes can tell you a lot about what you are experiencing. When you're anxious or angry, you may find the breath to be shallow and rapid. When you are resting, the breath slows down and is often deeper. The relationship between the breath, the body, and the mind goes both ways. By breathing more deeply, you are telling the nervous system you are safe. This exercise engages the parasympathetic nervous system, which is responsible for feelings of safety, relaxation, and ease.

STEPS

1   You can use this practice anytime. It works well when you are experiencing anxiety, anger, or any other emotion that increases the heart rate.

2   Bring the breath into your awareness. You can choose one place in the body on which to focus. The abdomen and chest work well for this exercise. ➤

3   For the first minute or so, breathe in for three seconds and breathe out for four. Do your best to count the seconds in your head.

4   Make the breath a bit longer by inhaling to a count of four and exhaling to a count of five.

5   After a minute or two, continue to lengthen the breath. Breathe in for five seconds and breathe out for seven seconds. Keep your attention on the sensation in the body as you breathe.

6   As the minutes pass, lengthen your inhales and exhales as much as you're able. Don't strain, but encourage yourself to breathe more deeply. Remember that the exhale should be longer than the inhale.

7   After 10 minutes, let go of the counting and take a few deep breaths at your own pace. Return to your day without returning to shallow breathing right away.

60
Caring for the Difficulty

TIME: 10 MINUTES

When we are faced with a difficult emotion, we often seek ways to change how we feel, trying to "outthink" the emotional experience or putting our attention elsewhere. Attending to these moments with mindfulness requires some patience and compassion. By caring for the painful experience, you can allow yourself to feel it and see it with clarity. This exercise will help you practice being with the difficulty rather than pushing it away.

STEPS

1 Start this practice when you are experiencing something difficult. It can be an emotional experience, such as anger; a mental experience, like racing thoughts; an external experience, like a stressful workday; or any other difficulty you face during your day.

2 When you notice that you're having a difficult moment, bring your awareness into the experience. Instead of pushing it away or resisting, turn toward it.

3 Place your hand over your heart. This stimulates the vagus nerve, activating the parasympathetic nervous system. ➤

4   Recognizing the pain and keeping your hand on your heart, offer yourself a few phrases. These phrases help you recognize the difficulty, turn toward it, and respond with compassion:

> *This is a moment of pain [or discomfort, difficulty, etc.]*
>
> *I cannot avoid all pain in life.*
>
> *I care about this suffering.*

5   Repeat these phrases to yourself with the intention of caring for the difficulty. If the mind tries to fix the pain or solve the problem, just return to the phrases and self-compassion.

6   After 10 minutes, let go of the phrases and remove the hand from the chest. The difficulty may not be gone, but remember the phrases are always accessible throughout your day.

61
Tender Heart for Others

TIME: 15 MINUTES

Humans are social creatures, which can be beautiful when we all get along. Other times, people can cause us harm or push our buttons. The heart builds a barrier, closing itself off slightly in order to protect us and ensure our safety and happiness.

Instead of closing the heart, you can open the heart and train it to respond with care for those who frustrate you. This is a practice in loving-kindness and recognition of the harm caused.

STEPS

1   As you close the eyes and settle into a comfortable meditation posture, bring loving-kindness to the mind and body. Without straining, allow yourself to gently settle into present-time awareness.

2   Bring somebody to mind whom you find difficult. If it is your first time using this exercise, try choosing somebody who's just mildly challenging. It may be someone who pushes your buttons or whom you find frustrating for some reason. ➤

3   Reflect on the fact that this is a person who is subject to the emotional experiences of joy, love, sorrow, and grief, just like you. Start by picturing the person with a smile across their face.

4   Begin offering a few phrases of appreciative joy, remembering that the intention with the practice is to open your own heart to care for this person's happiness. Use these phrases:

May you be happy.

May your happiness continue.

May I be happy for you.

5   After a few minutes, imagine this person experiencing pain or sorrow. Notice any response in your mind or body as you do so. Begin offering a few phrases of compassion for this person's difficulties. It is okay if you do not feel these phrases entirely. Offer them as much as you're able to in this moment.

May you be free from suffering.

I see your pain.

I care about your pain.

6   Finally, bring to mind what it is that you find difficult about the person. Tune in to the response of the mind and body as you bring the difficulty up. Respond with a few phrases of compassion for yourself, setting the intention to care for the unpleasant experience.

May I be free from suffering.

May I see my pain clearly.

May I respond with compassion.

62

Forgiving Faults

TIME: 15 MINUTES

The word *resentment* comes from Latin roots. Its original meaning was "to feel again." We all deal with resentments, holding on to harm that has been caused in the past. This is a painful experience. When you hold on like this, you feel the pain repeatedly.

Sometimes these resentments may feel like they offer security from future harm. But with forgiveness, you can free up space in the heart to allow love and care to take root. The practice of forgiveness will help you let go of these painful experiences and offer freedom to the mind and heart.

STEPS

1 Find a comfortable meditation posture and invite gentleness into the body from the beginning. Notice any discomfort or tension in the body and try to soften around it. ➤

2   Bring to mind somebody you feel resentful toward. When new to this practice, don't choose the strongest resentment in your heart. Instead, start where it's a little bit easier. Notice the harm that was caused and why you feel resentful.

3   Connect with the intention to cultivate an open and loving heart. If there is resistance, notice its presence without pushing it away. It takes time to reopen the heart, so don't force anything.

4   Begin offering phrases of forgiveness, connecting with the words as much as you are able. Say a phrase slowly in your head, finding a rhythm. It may be helpful to offer a phrase with each exhale or with every other exhale. Use these phrases:

I forgive you [or I forgive you as much as I am able to in this moment].

May I let this pain free itself from my heart.

5   After six or seven minutes of offering forgiveness, let go of these phrases. Turn toward yourself, recognizing that you, too, have caused harm to others. You don't need to engage in stories about the harm you have caused; just recognize that you have indeed caused difficulties for others, whether you intended to or not. Call to mind a specific person you have hurt. Begin asking for forgiveness from this person, using these phrases:

I ask for forgiveness for any harm I have caused you.

May you find room in your heart to forgive me.

May you forgive one another.

6   Allow five minutes to pass, and return to your own body. Breathe deeply for a few minutes, resting your awareness on the breath before opening the eyes.

SAFETY AND FORGIVENESS

When you work on forgiveness, it may feel like you are being weak or opening yourself up to future harm. Remember that forgiveness does not require you to let somebody back into your life, to let them cause harm again, or to be okay with somebody's actions. You can let go of the resentment while still retaining healthy boundaries. A forgiving heart sets boundaries out of self-care, while a resentful heart sets boundaries out of fear.

RAIN

I'm not sure where this practice originated, but I learned it during my teacher training with psychologist and meditation teacher Tara Brach. RAIN stands for Recognize, Allow (or Accept), Investigate, Nourish. This is one of my personal go-to practices. You can use it with any experience, make it a stand-alone meditation practice, and return to it with ease in daily life. It is especially helpful with difficult emotions and thoughts.

STEPS

1   Sit comfortably and begin bringing your awareness to your present-time experience. Give yourself a minute or two after closing the eyes to notice what you hear, what you feel in the body, and what is occurring in the mind.

2   Bringing up a difficult experience or emotion, start with recognition. Recognize the thoughts coming up, the sensations in the body, and the critical inner voice you often hear. Spend a few minutes just acknowledging the presence of the difficulty, tuning in to the different ways it manifests in your experience.

3   Move to the next phase: allowance or acceptance. With unpleasant emotions, the habit of the mind is to try to get rid of these experiences. Instead, allow it to be present in you. You may try offering this simple phrase of equanimity and acceptance: "Right now, it's like this." Continue to work with acceptance for five minutes, bringing the mind back when it starts pushing the difficulty away.

4   Now begin investigating more deeply. You recognized what you were feeling in the first step of RAIN. In investigation, allow curiosity to take over. Ask yourself where you feel vulnerable, how this emotion serves you, and if you believe you can be free from this pain.

5   For the final five minutes, turn toward nourishing yourself with self-compassion. This whole exercise has been a practice of self-compassion, as you are tending to the pain with awareness rather than denying it. However, make a dedicated effort to offer a few phrases of compassion and open the heart.

NON-IDENTIFICATION: *Another common use of the final N in RAIN is non-identification. Although not as heartfelt as the word* nourish, *it offers a powerful practice, as well. You can move through the practice as described, but when you get to the end, practice letting go of the experience. Recognize that this thought or experience is not* you, *or even* yours. *It is an impermanent process, arising and passing as all experiences do. Let it go.*

5-4-3-2-1

When you are in the throes of an overwhelming emotion, it can hook you in completely. Mindfulness practice helps you notice when this happens. When you do notice you are feeling over-whelmed, you can use this exercise to bring yourself back to the here and now. It takes just a few minutes and extends an invitation to be present.

STEPS

1 Leaving the eyes open, notice five things you can see. You can say them out loud or silently in your head. With each of the five sights, pause to take them in completely.

2 Next, notice four things you can feel in the body. Note them out loud or in your head, and rest your attention with each sensation for a few deep breaths.

3 Name three things you can hear. Try to choose three different sounds, not the same noise three times.

4   Note two things you can smell. If you cannot seem to smell two things in this moment, feel free to move somewhere to smell something more closely.

5   Finally, find one thing you can taste. It may be the leftover taste of a meal, your toothpaste, or just your breath. If you cannot connect with one in the moment, note a taste you enjoy in general.

65

You Can Handle This

You are capable of handling more than you give yourself credit for. Difficult emotions may sometimes get the better of you, but they always pass, and you always make it through them. By bringing mindfulness to the process of going through hard times, you can train yourself to recognize your own resilience. Seeing clearly that you are capable of handling the difficulty, you will train the mind to know you are okay.

STEPS

1   Close the eyes and adjust your posture so that you are comfortable. Ground yourself in the body, feeling the feet on the floor, the body in the chair or cushion, and the movement with the breath.

2   Bring to mind a difficult emotion you have experienced recently. Do not indulge in the story. Instead, focus on the feeling. You can do this by tuning in first to the body. What does the body feel like when this emotion is present?

3   Feeling the emotion in the body, investigate your capacity to be with it. What feels overwhelming or unmanageable? Ask yourself if you are able to handle the feeling in this single moment. Continue to tend to the bodily experience, examining whether you're able to be present with it or not.

4   After a few minutes, move your attention to the mind and mental state. When this emotion is present, what is the mind doing? Notice the thoughts that arise and the general feeling of the mind. Again, ask yourself if anything arising is too much for you to handle.

5   For the final two minutes, reflect on the pains and difficulties you have gone through over your life. Through small frustrations and larger experiences of grief and tragedy, you have made it to this moment, today. Recognize your natural resiliency, remembering that you are, indeed, capable.

66

Having a Bad Day

TIME: 15 MINUTES

We all have those days where nothing seems to be going our way. You may be feeling under the weather, emotionally exhausted, or overwhelmed with responsibilities. Labeling the day as a "bad day" may feel right, but it is often inaccurate—no day is 100 percent bad; there is almost always *something* good, however small. You can train the mind to recognize both the good and the bad, helping you see clearly that there are likely also pleasant and enjoyable moments during the day and that none of these moments is permanent. When you do have painful moments, you can respond with compassion and rewrite the story of the day.

STEPS

1 This practice works well when you are in the midst of a difficult day. Find a quiet place and a few minutes to sit in silence.

2 Closing the eyes, begin by settling into the body. Feel yourself sitting still, the connection of the body with the chair or cushion, and the movement in the body related to breathing.

3 Bring to mind something difficult you have experienced today. Use a specific event, a general feeling, or whatever arises naturally in the mind.

4 As the feeling of your "bad day" arises, pay attention to what that experience is like. Notice if there is a feeling in the body or any thought processes in the mind. Steer clear of picking it apart too much; instead, tune in to the overall experience and emotion. Ask yourself how it feels to be having a tough time today.

5 With awareness of how this feels, begin offering yourself some compassion. Retain some awareness on the experience in the mind and the body. You can silently offer these phrases:

This is a moment of pain [or difficulty, discomfort, or suffering].

May I tend to this pain with caring awareness.

6 After five minutes of offering compassion to yourself, let go of the phrases. Bring something to mind that has brought you joy or contentment today. See if you can find a moment in which you weren't enveloped by the discomfort or pain. It may be when you first woke up, a nice conversation with a friend or coworker, or the time you were eating lunch and not focused on the difficulties.

7 As something comes to mind, connect with how the experience felt. Recognize that although you may be having a hard day, here is a moment of freedom from the pain. Offer the simple phrase "May I appreciate this moment." ➤

8   Continue bringing to mind other times in which you experienced some contentment during your day. As each new one comes up, sit with it for a few deep breaths and repeat the phrase. As you run low on pleasant or enjoyable experiences, look for the neutral moments in your day.

9   As you finish the practice, reflect for a minute on the whole of your day. Without denying your own experience of having a bad day, also recognize that the entire day was not unpleasant. Tune in to the fact that many moments were pleasant or neutral.

67

Liking Yourself

TIME: 10 MINUTES

The self-talk you engage in regularly is often unkind. You beat yourself up, hold yourself to unrealistic standards, and focus on how to always be better. With mindfulness, you can tune in to this voice and acknowledge these thoughts.

You can also learn to tune in to the things you like about yourself. Even if they aren't obvious in every moment, there *are* parts of you that you like. In this exercise, you will bring your awareness to these aspects of yourself to offer a more complete picture of who you are.

STEPS

1 Close the eyes and find a comfortable posture in which to sit. Bring your awareness to the sensation of the body breathing. You can focus on the chest, abdomen, or nostrils. For the first few minutes, allow the mind to settle and focus by returning your attention to the breath as many times as necessary. ➤

2 Once the mind has settled, begin by bringing something to mind that you appreciate about yourself. Start with the body. Ask yourself what you like about your body, and just pause to appreciate it for a moment. It may be a physical feature, like your hair or skin, or it may be a quality, like strength or flexibility. As something arises, stay with the experience of liking this part of yourself for a few breaths.

3 After a minute or two of working with the body, switch to the mind. Look at the qualities of your brain and emotional experience. Ask yourself what you appreciate about your brain, your insight, and your personality. Again, simply be with the appreciation when something arises.

4 For the last few minutes, focus on the five traditional senses: sight, smell, taste, hearing, and touch. Go through each sense, recognizing the beauty and pleasure these senses have brought you. For example, recognize that your sense of hearing has allowed you to hear the voice of a loved one. The sense of touch has allowed you to feel the comfort of a hug. Be with each sense, what gifts it brings you, and the appreciation.

ACKNOWLEDGING THE CRITIC

Whether it is during this practice or in your daily life, you may notice your inner critic running background commentary on your present experience. Remember that you don't have to believe every thought you have, and the more you can bring that background noise into the light, the less power it will have. Try thanking the thought for its input and then leaving it be. Don't push it away; allow it to arise and pass on its own. Mindfully recognize the thoughts that come up, and be grateful to yourself for getting familiar with your thought patterns.

68

Recognizing Needs

TIME: 15 MINUTES

When you begin tuning in mindfully to your experience, you may also start to notice your difficulties and struggles. Part of mindfulness is recognizing what you need in these moments. I invite you to respond in a way that promotes your well-being and freedom and not in a way that perpetuates your pain and suffering. This exercise offers a concrete way to pause and look at your needs in a given moment.

STEPS

1 Sit up as straight as you are able, and gently close the eyes. For this practice, it is helpful to start with a few minutes of concentration practice to truly settle. Pick a location in the body where you can feel the body breathing, and tune in to the sensations of the breath for a couple of minutes.

2 Bring to mind a recent situation that you found difficult or painful. Without falling too far into the story, acknowledge how this experience feels in the present moment. ➤

3   With the memory and experience present in your consciousness, ask yourself what you needed in that moment. Focus on general emotional needs, like compassion, understanding, and insight. With this difficulty, what would have helped you? When a need pops up, say to yourself, "I needed _____." Continue to tune in to other needs, really pausing to acknowledge each one.

4   After five minutes, turn your awareness to your experience in the present. Refraining from stories and goals, ask yourself what you need right now. Let go of thoughts about getting stuff done, completing tasks, and pleasing others. Focus on your deeper needs of self-care, patience, or whatever is true for you in this moment.

5   Wrapping up this exercise, reflect on your own capacity to meet your needs. Can you do something to meet those needs right now? Are there any needs you have that are not within your power to fulfill? Offer yourself self-care, compassion, and patience.

69
Self-Supporting

TIME: 15 MINUTES

As the mind and body take cues from one another, we can use our own hands to encourage states of ease and comfort. This is a practice I learned from Nancy Napier, a leading psychotherapist who works with those who have experienced trauma. The basic premise is that the human body responds to touch, and touch can change the activity in the nervous system. I recommend familiarizing yourself with these practices, then utilizing them in your daily life when you need a way to calm down.

STEPS

1   Sit in a comfortable position and close the eyes. Breathe deeply through the nostrils, allowing the lungs to fully empty with the exhale. Continue breathing deeply for a minute.

2   Spend a few minutes bringing awareness to the body in this moment. Without changing or fixing anything, observe what is present. Notice what physical sensations you can feel and where you can feel them. Try to really drop your awareness out of your head and down into the body. ➤

3 Begin supporting yourself by bringing one of the hands to the top of the opposite arm, just below the shoulder. Gently rest the hand here with the intention of offering yourself support. This is a place of support in the human body. Allow yourself to feel the care and support you have for yourself. Tune in to any relaxation in the mind or body.

4 After a few minutes, release the hand. Take a few deep breaths and bring the hand to the back of the head, where the spine meets the skull. This is a place where you were held and supported as an infant, and it can offer a sense of safety and ease. As you gently rest the hand here, allow the body to feel safe and comfortable.

5 Allowing a few minutes to pass, move the hand to the center of the chest. This stimulates the vagus nerve, releasing oxytocin and engaging the parasympathetic nervous system. Allow the hand to rest here, feeling care for yourself as you relax the body and mind.

6 After a couple of minutes with the hand on the chest, allow the hand to relax once again. Let a few minutes pass while you breathe and invite in relaxation to the mind and body before opening the eyes.

BRINGING THIS PRACTICE TO LIFE: *You can use any of these practices in daily life whenever you are struggling. They are especially helpful when you are feeling overly activated. This may be from anxiety, stress, anger, or any other emotional experience that gets the nervous system going. Recognizing this with mindfulness, you can respond with these acts of self-compassion. Take a moment to rest your hand on your upper arm with the intention of supporting yourself.*

70

The Pelvis Bowl

TIME: 10 MINUTES

There are many ways you can settle the mind down when it becomes active. This exercise is one I use frequently to encourage relaxation in the mind and body when I am overwhelmed. You may use it as a stand-alone practice, to return to the body during the day, or at the beginning of a meditation period to help yourself settle.

STEPS

1 Allow the eyes to close, and sit with the spine as straight as possible. Use the breath to encourage a gentle awareness. With the inhalation, reach the spine upward. With the exhalation, let go. Let the shoulders drop, relax the jaw, and soften the belly. ➤

2   After a minute or two of breathing like this, turn your attention to the pelvis and hips. Picture this part of the body as a bowl. As you exhale, allow all of the body's energy to slowly fall into the bowl. Feel the stability of the bowl sitting on the chair or cushion, and let the body relax into this bowl.

3   Continue with your awareness on the pelvis, allowing the body to really relax. Similar to Exercise 12, Caring for Yourself (page 30), you can think of the body like a snow globe. After the snow globe has been shaken, it takes time and patience to let each snowflake settle. As you sit, allow the body to relax and settle with a patient awareness. With each exhale, allow the body to soften.

71

Where Is My Mind?

TIME: 15 MINUTES

Simply by bringing awareness to the mind, you naturally detach from its thoughts and meanderings. When you observe your own thoughts, you naturally create a separation from them, because you see that they often arise on their own. In this way, you are not as likely to get sucked into each thought. You can notice individual thoughts, overarching mental states, or how active or dull the mind is in any given moment.

This practice offers yet another way to understand the thinking mind. You will use a simple noting exercise to look at where the mind is as thoughts arise. Rather than focusing on the content of the thoughts themselves, you will tune in to their general context.

STEPS

1 Close the eyes and adjust the body to find a comfortable and sustainable posture. As you will be working with thoughts, it is helpful to dedicate the first five minutes to building concentration. Choose a place in the body and rest the awareness on the breath. When the mind wanders, simply bring it back with kindness to the experience of breathing. ➤

2   Open your awareness to the mind and thought processes. Using the breath as your anchor, stay with the sensation of breathing until a thought comes up. When you notice a thought arise, note what its general context is. Rather than tuning in to the specifics of the thought, note whether it is rumination, problem solving, fantasizing, or another thinking pattern.

3   When you recognize you are thinking, note the thought and return to the breath. Patiently sit with the body breathing, waiting for another thought to arise. Again, note what the thought is in general without diving into specifics or getting wrapped up in it.

4   After five minutes or so, you may consider adding in an additional piece. Note whether the thought is about the past, present, or future. Without labeling one as good or another as bad, just note where the mind is.

5   As you come out of this practice, try to retain some awareness of the thinking mind. Going about daily tasks, recognize when the mind is off and wandering. Try noting where the mind is when you see this happening.

72

Kindness with Thoughts

TIME: 15 MINUTES

You may notice that your response to the mind and its thoughts is not always rooted in kindness and gentleness. Traditionally, loving-kindness is practiced toward a person (even if that person is yourself), but you can direct this same sentiment toward the mind itself. With practice, you can learn to respond to the mind with greater acceptance. This helps you see more clearly and not get caught up in reacting to each and every thought.

STEPS

1   Sit in a way that feels healthy and conducive to mindfulness. Listen to your body and make any adjustments to find a comfortable posture.

2   As with the previous exercise, begin with a few minutes of concentration practice. Bring your attention to the body breathing, and gently train the mind to focus. ➤

3   Open up to your thoughts. Keeping your awareness of the breath as your anchor, simply notice when a thought arises. You may label it or note its contents, but focus on responding to it with gentleness. Whether the thought is pleasant, unpleasant, or neutral, try to bring some patience to the thinking mind.

4   When a thought arises, offer a phrase of loving-kindness toward the mind and the thought. You may try using one of these phrases:

May I be at ease with the mind.

May I be at ease with this thought.

Thinking mind, gentle mind.

5   Reconnect with the intention to respond to your thoughts with kindness over and over again. When the mind wanders off, just come back to the breath and pay attention when a thought comes up. Gently offer a phrase of loving-kindness and return to your desire to be at ease with the mind. You may even try offering a phrase to the wandering itself.

6   When you complete this practice, make a dedicated effort to carry it with you during your day. Pause and offer the mind and thoughts a few phrases of loving-kindness when you're waiting in line, walking to your car, or checking the mail.

73

The Strong You

TIME: 10 MINUTES

I lived for a few years across from a building covered in street art by the Los Angeles artist Chase. He uses the slogan "Remember who you are" on many of the pieces he creates, a beautiful reminder to reconnect with who you are underneath all the stories. Every day when I walked past the art-covered building, I used it as a cue to reconnect with myself.

This exercise offers a way to deeply reconnect. Although it is not a traditional mindfulness practice, you can use it to remember who you are, especially when you forget.

STEPS

1   Sitting in a comfortable posture, close the eyes and take a few deep breaths through the nostrils.

2   Imagine yourself in a difficult situation. It may be something coming up that is bringing some fear or anxiety or something you went through in the recent past. Recognize any fear or aversion that is present as you bring this event to mind. Maybe you want to ask for a raise, need to have a difficult conversation with a loved one, or have an upcoming appointment that is bringing some worry. ➤

3 Rather than playing out the story in your head, ask yourself what the strongest version of yourself would do and how *they* would handle it. Picture your strong self handling the situation with complete kindness, care, mindfulness, patience, and wisdom.

4 As you visualize this situation in your head, make special effort to notice the strength within you. Allow yourself to feel strong and confident. When you begin doubting yourself, return back to the strong you. Reconnect with your intentions of wisdom and compassion in the face of difficulties.

5 You can continue with one experience, playing it through multiple times. You can also try working with a different situation or event. Continue to connect with the strength you have within you. Remember to breathe deeply and watch for any anxiety and worry.

6 When you finish this practice, you may try writing about your experience. Writing after this exercise gives you a crystallized look at yourself as the strong you, and can help clarify how you are able to handle painful experiences.

ACTING OUT OF STRENGTH: *When the situation arrives and it is time for you to go into the difficulty, remember who you are. Reconnect with the strong you for a few moments. You can close your eyes and quickly return to your visualization for a few moments to connect with the mindfulness, compassion, and wisdom you intend to bring to your life. Remind yourself that you are capable of meeting this situation with wisdom.*

74

Space for Feeling

TIME: 10 MINUTES

It's common to tighten around your discomfort. You tense the body when you are struggling, trying to rid yourself of the unpleasantness. Instead of tightening, you can make room for the pain. Welcoming it in and meeting it with a caring presence, you have the power to retrain the mind. This helps you build a nonreactive awareness. Rather than being controlled by every challenging situation, you can notice it, allow it to be present, and move forward.

STEPS

1   For this practice, find a comfortable position. You may investigate doing this exercise sitting or lying down.

2   Give yourself a few minutes to settle. Breathe deeply, allowing the mind and body to relax with each exhale. Without ignoring the unpleasantness, invite in calmness. ➤

3 Pay attention to the painful emotion you are experiencing. Don't fall into the story. Recognize how the mind and body feel right now. Ask if it is sadness, fear, frustration, or disappointment. Just notice the general tone and experience you are feeling.

4 Begin making space for the emotion by offering a few phrases of compassion. Remember your intention to care for the pain rather than push it away. Offer these phrases to the pain or difficulty:

You are welcome here.

There is space for you.

May I welcome you with compassion.

5 Continue to offer the phrases for five minutes or so, reconnecting with your intention to tend to the experience with an open and caring heart.

6 As you wrap up, return to the breath for a minute or two. With each exhale, soften the body. Let the shoulders drop down, allow the jaw to relax, and soften the muscles in the abdomen.

75

Letting Go of Fixing

TIME: 10 MINUTES

When there is discontentment, the natural habit is to correct it. The mind goes into "fix-it" mode. This often results in circular thinking, trying in vain to solve a problem. Although reflection and goal setting are useful, the obsession you experience is often not.

This exercise offers a technique to work with this "fix-it" thinking. You can use it in a formal meditation practice and return to it at any point during your day when you notice the mind stuck on a loop of problem solving.

STEPS

1 Sit up as straight as possible, inviting alertness into the mind and body. Take a few deep breaths, energizing the body.

2 Begin to tune in to your thoughts. What problem are you working to solve? Is there something specific you want to figure out or fix? Notice the issue itself, not your thoughts about it. Try to clearly see what the problem is, rather than focusing on the solution. ➤

3   With the "problem" in your mind, notice any discomfort you feel around
    it. There may be some fear of the unknown, insecurity, or a desire to plan
    something. Whatever your experience is, look at the issue with tender
    awareness. There's no need to judge yourself, beat yourself up, or jump
    right into fixing. Just be with the discomfort.

4   As you rest in awareness of the problem to be solved, begin tuning in
    to the mind and body. Is there tension in the body? Notice where it is.
    Recognize when the mind jumps into the desire to fix the discomfort
    by saying to yourself, "Fixing."

5   With the intention of meeting your experience with patience, offer
    yourself a few phrases of mindful care:

    I see this discomfort.

    The mind wants to fix it.

    May I be with this problem.

6   To close this meditation, take a minute to ask yourself what can be done.
    You don't need to come up with a clear, step-by-step plan. Just offer the
    simplest solution possible. For example, if you're worried about bills,
    recognize that you may need to save some money. Allow a basic solution
    to arise, and don't dive more deeply into the story.

Resources

Here are some tools that I use in my own practice. These resources will help you continue your practice and find support as you do so.

BOOKS

A Burning Desire: Dharma God and the Path of Recovery by Kevin Griffin
A Fierce Heart: Finding Strength, Courage, and Wisdom in Any Moment by Spring Washam
A Path with Heart: A Guide through the Perils and Promises of Spiritual Life by Jack Kornfield
Breath by Breath: The Liberating Practice of Insight Meditation by Larry Rosenberg with David Guy
Buddha's Brain: The Practical Neuroscience of Happiness, Love, and Wisdom by Rick Hanson with Richard Mendius
The Miracle of Mindfulness: An Introduction to the Practice of Meditation by Thich Nhat Hanh
Radical Acceptance: Embracing Your Life with the Heart of a Buddha by Tara Brach
Real Happiness: The Power of Meditation by Sharon Salzberg

WEBSITES

Access to Insight – www.accesstoinsight.org
Dr. Kristin Neff – self-compassion.org
Greater Good Magazine – greatergood.berkeley.edu
Mindful – www.mindful.org
Mindful Schools – www.mindfulschools.org

Tricycle Magazine – tricycle.org
Wildmind – www.wildmind.org

Calm – www.calm.com
Headspace – www.headspace.com
Insight Timer – www.insighttimer.com
MetaFi – www.metafi.me
10% Happier – www.10percenthappier.com

Against the Stream – www.againstthestream.org/podcasts/
Audio Dharma – www.audiodharma.org
Buddhist Geeks – www.buddhistgeeks.org
Dharma Seed – www.dharmaseed.org
Greater Good Science Center – greatergood.berkeley.edu/podcasts
Metta Hour – www.sharonsalzberg.com/metta-hour-podcast/
Secular Buddhist Association – secularbuddhism.org/category/podcasts
Tara Brach – www.tarabrach.com/talks-audio-video/
10% Happier – www.10percenthappier.com/podcast

Against the Stream/Dharma Punx – www.againstthestream.org
East Bay Meditation Center – eastbaymeditation.org
Insight Meditation Center – www.insightmeditationcenter.org
Insight Meditation Community of Washington – imcw.org
Insight Meditation Society – www.dharma.org
InsightLA – insightla.org
Spirit Rock – www.spiritrock.org
Vipassana – www.dhamma.org

References

Baraz, James, and Shoshana Alexander. *Awakening Joy: 10 Steps to Happiness.* Berkeley, CA: Parallax Press, 2012.

Bodhipaksa. "Why the Emphasis on Concentration?" Wildmind Buddhist Meditation. February 13, 2007. https://www.wildmind.org/mindfulness /four/concentrate.

Boorstein, Sylvia. *Don't Just Do Something, Sit There: A Mindfulness Retreat with Sylvia Boorstein.* San Francisco: HarperOne, 1996.

Brach, Tara. *True Refuge: Finding Peace and Freedom in Your Own Awakened Heart.* New York: Bantam Books, 2013.

Chödrön, Pema. "The Breath of Compassion." Awaken. November 18, 2016. http://www.awaken.com/2016/11/the-breath-of-compassion/.

Claiborne, Craig. *The New York Times Cookbook.* New York: Harper & Row, 1961.

Corliss, Julie. "Mindfulness Meditation Helps Fight Insomnia, Improves Sleep." *Harvard Health Blog.* last modified December 22, 2015. https://www .health.harvard.edu/blog/mindfulness-meditation-helps-fight-insomnia -improves-sleep-201502187726.

Dillbeck, Michael C. "Meditation and Flexibility of Visual Perception and Verbal Problem Solving." *Memory & Cognition* 10, no. 3 (May 1982): 207–15. https://doi.org/10.3758/BF03197631.

Hanson, Rick. *Buddha's Brain: The Practical Neuroscience of Happiness, Love, and Wisdom.* Oakland, CA: New Harbinger, 2009.

———. *Hardwiring Happiness: The New Brain Science of Contentment, Calm, and Confidence.* New York: Harmony Books, 2013.

Hofmann, Stefan G., Alice T. Sawyer, Ashley A. Witt, and Diana Oh. "The Effect of Mindfulness-Based Therapy on Anxiety and Depression: A Meta-Analytic Review." *Journal of Consulting and Clinical Psychology* 78, no. 2 (April 2010): 169–83. doi:10.1037/a0018555.

Hughes, J. W., D. M. Fresco, R. Myerscough, M. H. M. van Dulmen, L. E. Carlson, and R. Josephson. "Randomized Controlled Trial of Mindfulness-Based Stress Reduction for Prehypertension." *Psychosomatic Medicine* 75, no. 8 (October 2013): 721–28. doi:10.1097/PSY.0b013e3182a3e4e5.

Mrazek, Michael D., Michael S. Franklin, Dawa Tarchin Phillips, Benjamin Baird, and Jonathan W. Schooler. "Mindfulness Training Improves Working Memory Capacity and GRE Performance While Reducing Mind Wandering." *Psychological Science* 24, no. 5 (May 2013): 776–81. doi:10.1177/0956797612459659.

Nouwen, Henri J. M. *The Inner Voice of Love: A Journey through Anguish to Freedom.* New York: Doubleday, 1996.

Rattue, Grace. "Meditation Can Help Loneliness." *Medical News Today.* August 17, 2012. https://www.medicalnewstoday.com/articles/249181.php.

Sayadaw, Mahasi. *Manual of Insight.* Edited by Steve Armstrong. Translated by Vipassana Metta Foundation Translation Committee. Somerville, MA: Wisdom Publications, 2016.

Watts, Alan. *The Essence of Alan Watts.* Millbrae, CA: Celestial Arts, 1977.

Index

N

Napier, Nancy, 157
Needs, 155–156
Negativity bias, 101
Nhat Hanh, Thich, xi, 12, 131
Non-identification, 145
Noting, xxv
  Breathing and Noting, 63
  The Judgment-Free Zone, 43–44
Nouwen, Henri, 91

O

Open-Awareness Meditation, 61–62
Open mindfulness, 61–62

P

Pain, xiii. *See also* Emotions
  Caring for the Difficulty, 137–138
  Forgiving Faults, 141–143
  Having a Bad Day, 150–152
  Recognizing Needs, 155–156
  Smiling, 131–132
  Space for Feeling, 167–168
  Stopping Rumination, 123–124
Parasympathetic nervous system, xxv
  Extending the Exhale, 135–136
  Where Are the Feet? 93–94
Patience, xiv, 14
  Shopping Mindfully, 95–96
  What Are You Waiting For? 105–106
Pelvis Bowl, The, 159–160
People Are People, 103–104
Phrases, xxv, 22
Physical body. *See also* Senses
  Bedtime Mindfulness, 17
  Body Awareness, 26–27
  Calming the Body, 119–120
  Mindful Bathing, 89–90
  The Mindful Body, 20–22
  The Pelvis Bowl, 159–160
  Scanning the Body, 15–17
  Self-Supporting, 157
  What Is This Emotion? 127–128

Where Are the Feet? 93–94
Physical health, xviii
Points of Contact, 5–7
Positivity, 101–102
Post-traumatic stress disorder, xv
Power of the Mind, The, 8–9
Present-time experience, xxv
  Doing the Dishes, 77–78
  Mindful Cleaning, 79–80
  Points of Contact, 5–7
  Scanning the Body, 15–17
Problem solving, xviii, 169–170

Q

Qualities, cultivating, 32

R

RAIN, 144–145
Recognizing Needs, 155–156
Relaxation
  Calming the Body, 119–120
  Extending the Exhale, 135–136
  Resting the Mind, 41–42
Releasing the Pressure Valve, 125–126
Resentment, 141
Resilience, xiv
  The Strong You, 165–166
  You Can Handle This, 148–149
Resting the Mind, 41–42
Rumi, 30
Rumination, 123–124

S

Scanning the Body, 15–17
Seeing, 85–86
Self-esteem, xix
Self-judgment, 25, 44
Self-Supporting, 157–158
Self-talk, 153
Sense-doors, xxv
Senses
  Color Your World, 85–86
  Cooking with Clarity, 73–74
  Eating Mindfully, 12–14

Acknowledgments

This book was inspired by my own practice, and my practice has been inspired and supported by many people over the years. First and foremost, I want to deeply thank Elizabeth for the unconditional love she offered during my writing of this book, the support she gives me every day, and the consistent motivation to dive deeper.

I am grateful for all of the people who encouraged me to practice in my early years and saw me through the difficulties. I am forever appreciative of my parents and two sisters, who loved me when I was not able to love myself.

Thank you to the countless teachers in my life, especially Richard Burr, Noah Levine, Kevin Griffin, and Thanissaro Bhikkhu. You have continually strengthened my practice and given me direction on this path.

Thank you to our wonderful community at One Mind Dharma, which has strengthened my practice and given me a community. You fill my heart with love and my mind with wisdom every day.

Finally, I owe a deep debt of gratitude to those who held my hand with love as I began this journey: Vogi, who always knows when to lovingly push me forward and taught me what it means to be an adult, and Jack, who went above and beyond to act with love and compassion. I simply would not be here without you, and I know you would have been the first ones to read the book.

About the Author

MATTHEW SOCKOLOV is a meditation teacher in Petaluma, California. The founding teacher of One Mind Dharma, Matthew leads meditation groups at the center and works one-on-one with individuals across the country who wish to deepen their practice. He has worked for years with recovering addicts, adolescents, and those who join the community to practice. Trained as a Buddhist meditation teacher at Spirit Rock Insight Meditation Center, Matthew has worked closely with many teachers in the Theravada Buddhism and insight meditation traditions. He has studied with Kevin Griffin, Thanissaro Bhikkhu, and the community at Against the Stream. Matthew lives in Northern California with his wife, Elizabeth, teaching meditation, spending time outdoors, and enjoying time with his dog, cats, and chickens. You can find Matthew at MattSock.com. His meditations, free podcasts, and writing are available at OneMindDharma.com.

CPSIA information can be obtained
at www.ICGtesting.com
Printed in the USA
BVHW062251170620
581644BV00006B/11